MOVING A NATION TO CARE

"This book is an insider's look at the issues. It begs the question, "Are we honoring the sacrifices of the men and women who have served? Are we doing all that we can do to provide them with the tools to return to society." If this book creates debate in Congress or causes a parent to fight for the healthcare of their loved one, then it has accomplished its mission."—**Steve Robinson**, Director of Veterans Affairs, Veterans For America

"Ilona Meagher has done an impressive and important job in researching, assembling and chronicling the psychological suffering and neglect visited upon our new generation of veterans, their families and our nation. *Moving a Nation to Care* sounds a citizens' alarm to action on behalf of our veterans. We all must answer its call."—**Edward Tick**, Ph.D., Director of Soldier's Heart: A Veterans' Safe Return Initiative, and author of *War and the Soul, The Golden Tortoise* and *The Practice of Dream Healing*

"Going beyond mere yellow ribbons into the real support that returning troops need, this book is as easy to read as a newspaper and yet well-documented enough to keep on the shelf as a reference. We need to understand what we face, and this book does an excellent job of explaining that, along with what we can do to reduce the damage."—**Rachel M. MacNair,** author of *Perpetration-Induced Traumatic Stress: The Psychological Consequences of Killing*

"Ilona Meagher has been at the forefront of bringing the plight of veterans suffering from post-traumatic stress disorder to national attention. *Moving a Nation to Care* is a must read for anyone who understands that the worth of a nation is best measured by how it treats its wounded heroes."—Commander **Jeff Huber**, U.S. Navy (Retired)

"As the stories in *Moving A Nation To Care* illustrate, much work still remains if America is to fully heal the psychological wounds of war. Ilona Meagher's thorough and well documented research is a valuable resource for all those who truly want to support the troops."—**Mark Fleming**, Editor, *Unsolicited Opinion*

"PTSD is not a new phenomenon. But this painstakingly and footnoted researched guide reveals the little-recognized cost of the embedded pain and suffering wrought on returning U.S. troops by a high-tech, front-less, victory-less, faith-based, quagmire occupation of Iraq."—**Bill Densmore**, Director, The Media Giraffe Project at the University of Massachusetts—Amherst

MOVING A NATION TO CARE
POST-TRAUMATIC STRESS DISORDER AND AMERICA'S RETURNING TROOPS

ILONA MEAGHER

Brooklyn, New York

Printed in Canada
First Paperback Edition
10 9 8 7 6 5 4 3 2 1

Please direct inquiries to:
Ig Publishing
178 Clinton Avenue
Brooklyn, NY 11205
www.igpub.com

Library of Congress Cataloging-in-Publication Data

Meagher, Ilona.
    Moving a nation to care : post-traumatic stress disorder and America's returning
troops / by Ilona Meagher ; introduction by Penny Coleman.
       p. cm.
     ISBN-13: 978-0-9771972-7-9 (alk. paper)
     ISBN-10: 0-9771972-7-1
     1. Post-traumatic stress disorder--United States. 2. Iraq War, 2003---Veterans--Mental
health. 3. Afghan War, 2003---Veterans--Mental health. 4. Iraq War, 2003---Psychological
aspects. 5. Afghan War, 2003---Psychological aspects. 6. Veterans--Rehabilitation--United
States. 7. Veterans--Mental health--United States. 8. War--Psychological aspects.
I. Title.
     RC552.P67M43 2007
     616.85'212--dc22
                                   2007005216

CONTENTS

For Zsuzsanna
and our military families

FOREWORD

Our sons and daughters join the military to defend and protect us. Ask any military family what their loved ones mean to them and you will feel the human bonds that unite us in compassion for others. They are our husbands, wives, sons and daughters who form the very fabric of our society.

Wounds from the horror of war can produce a condition called post-traumatic stress disorder. When the hidden wounds of battle flare up from PTSD, it affects us all. We can try to look the other way and pretend there is no problem, but we cannot ignore the human suffering that arises from the personal tragedies of domestic violence, homicide and suicide that emerge as our returning soldiers attempt to re-integrate back into society.

We must do all we can to provide real support and help to those who gave so much. We need to raise our voices for a noble cause. We the people must make our wishes known to those who represent us in Congress. We must fight for those we believe in. In so doing we strengthen our children, our hopes, and ourselves and dreams.

Ilona Meagher has created a battle plan to help our active military, veterans and their families to truly come home. Her extensive research, personal interviews and networking with others dedicated to fighting for veterans has produced this powerful book.

Let us rally behind the troops with actions and deeds geared towards healing and hope. It is the American way.

Robert Roerich, M.D.
American Founder, Roadmind University Online
Vice President, National Gulf War Resource Center
Moderator, VeteranLove.com

INTRODUCTION

"Trouble is in the land. Confusion all around . . .
But I know, somehow, that only when it is dark enough,
can you see the stars."—Martin Luther King, Jr.

For members of the military and their families, America is a very troubled place right now. On top of enduring the anxiety of one or more combat deployments, upon their return home, these brave men and women are met not with compassion and support, but by a military culture that, in the face of all evidence, insists that their psychological injuries are a sign of weakness. Because of this, returning combat soldiers are discouraged from asking for help, and are forced to do battle with an under-funded bureaucracy in thrall to a partisan political agenda, and, perhaps most isolating of all, kept ignorant of an historical context that would help them understand that they are not alone in their struggles. For these soldiers and their families, as well as for the rest of us, *Moving a Nation to Care* is a point of light in an otherwise dark expanse.

When Jim Lehrer asked George Bush in January of this year why, if the outcome of the war in Iraq was of such transcendent importance to the future of our nation, had he not asked for greater sacrifice from the American people, Bush replied that Americans were sacrificing their peace of mind every time they turned on their televisions. But, in fact, the war our government has allowed us to see is bloodless and sanitized. On the eve of the invasion in 2003, the Pentagon issued a directive to the media forbidding any coverage of returning American coffins. That was just a prelude to the fantasy war Americans would experience at home, a war of non-existent WMDs, "spreading democracy," "shock and awe," "mission accomplished," "stay the course," and now, an unlikely "victory." The Bush administration's decision to institute a policy that Ilona Meagher rightly calls "public disengagement" has deprived us of the ability to see the truly staggering human costs of the war. With the exception of the unspeakable images of Abu Ghraib, which were in fact e-mailed home by soldiers themselves, we have only seen bits and pieces of a war that is being fought in a manner that would sicken most of us if we had full access. Vietnam-era images, like the naked child trying to outrun her own burning skin, or the anguished women and children waiting their turn to be executed at My Lai, were catalysts that helped turn public opinion against that war. Today, however, we have been deprived of the opportunity to check in with our consciences and our compassion. Americans are not a callous people, but the abstractions and the invisibility of this war have had a destructive and deadening impact. We are not asked for our opinions, and when we do offer them, we are accused of a lack of patriotism, of not supporting the troops.

Just as we have been insulated from the horror of what our troops are experiencing on the ground, we have also not been allowed to share the grief of their families when their loved ones arrive home with damaged bodies or minds or, worst of all, in a flag-draped box. Reporters have been denied access by the military to the stateside funerals of soldiers who have been killed in action, and Pentagon casualty reports disingenuously include only those troops injured by bullets or bombs, excluding accidental deaths, mental trauma and suicide. As a result, soldiers and their families have had to bear the cost of war by themselves, while the rest of us have been asked to sacrifice our most basic right as citizens: the right to participate.

Those of us who have tried to bring attention to the daunting number of war-related psychiatric casualties have been compromised in our efforts by a dearth of the kind of images and stories that would help us translate statistical information into human terms. I believe that one of the reasons we Americans have been so tolerant of what is being done in our names is that there have been so few human faces, voices and stories on which to hang our emotional understanding. That is one of the many gifts of Ilona's book, as *Moving a Nation to Care* offers vivid descriptions of individual soldiers and their combat experiences. The voices of our brave fighting men and women reveal the myriad ways in which war can undo a soldier's psyche, as well as bringing to life the sorrow and grief of family members who have tried, and sadly, too often failed, to help their traumatized loved ones find health and peace. The soldiers in this book speak to us of their all too personal experiences of inadequate screening and equipment, of the shortage of counseling and the irresponsible use of drugs, of the disregard for established military guidelines designed to protect their psychic health and of leaders who take no responsibility for the inevitable and often tragic consequences of this neglect. Their voices reveal the human cost of a cynical bottom-line policy to a public that has been kept in the dark. And we need just such an education. We need to be sensitized to the suffering of our soldiers before we can fully grasp what the experts are saying and before we can begin to do what we must do.

In addition to the contemporary tragedy, lessons of the past are also being ignored, lessons that should have been used in planning for what are, not surprisingly, the psychological casualties of warfare. Instead, we are being asked to accept PTSD as a new phenomenon, and to wait patiently while experts produce yet more studies that will certify once again that war injures soldiers in entirely predictable ways. To our great detriment, we are ignoring what we should have learned from the epidemic of traumatic stress injuries that showed up in Vietnam veterans, many of whom, left to manage their symptoms alone, without help and support, sabotaged their careers, ended up on the streets, homeless, often addicted, often violent, continuing to fight a war that has never ended for many of them. We are ignoring the truth that many will find it difficult to come home, and that some, finding it impossible, will choose death over the infinite anguish that has become their lives.

I know all about this, as my husband Daniel was one of them. There was no manual for care when Daniel returned from Vietnam in 1969, no one to warn me that the sweet gentle facade I fell in love with masked an interior turmoil that would emerge in bursts of confusing, unpredictable and self-destructive behavior. Daniel never talked about his war experiences, so when things got rough between us and he threatened to kill himself, I first thought the drama was romantic, then manipulative ... and then it was too late. No one knows how many other Vietnam veterans took their own lives in the aftermath of the war because nobody ever counted. To this day, the military still denies a relationship between PTSD and suicide.

Tragically, the same thing is happening again. The suicide rate among soldiers hit another high in 2006, and though veterans are mourned in their hometown papers, there is still no one tracking this, trying to find answers. This is obviously a job for the government and the military, but they haven't stepped up. No one has, except for Ilona Meagher, citizen journalist, blogger, creator of the *ePluribus Media PTSD Timeline* and now author of a book that will surely be a comfort to those whose lives have been touched by the trauma of war.

Moving A Nation to Care is the manual for care I wish I had been given thirty years ago. With it, maybe I would have been able to prevent what happened to Daniel, and to me. Even if that had not be possible, maybe I would not have felt so terribly alone in the aftermath, so consumed by guilt and shame that there was no room to grieve. This book offers more than a deep understanding of the nature of posttraumatic stress injuries, a saner approach to avoiding them and a thoroughly researched, selective resource guide for those who must learn to live with them. It is an invitation to, and a living example of, participation and advocacy. It asks that we listen to our soldiers and our veterans, and do our best to understand and empathize. It asks that we consider what we owe each other as citizens, and what we can do to build a society of conscience and compassion and justice. It asks us to reveal our very best nature by supporting our troops in ways that are truly meaningful to them and their families. Only out of that shared commitment, those reaffirmed loyalties and reexamined values, can our frayed social contract be renewed. *Moving A Nation to Care* is book filled with wisdom and love. It is truly a star in a troubled and confusing darkness.

Penny Coleman
March 2007

PREFACE

"War means something different to those of us that have looked through the sights of a rifle at another human being's face. Collateral damage means something different to those of us that have seen the lifeless body of a 9-year-old girl caught in the crossfire. Or for those of us that have struggled to save the life of a 7-year-old boy. I've only mentioned a fraction of what still haunts me from Iraq. I've been diagnosed with PTSD . . ." [1]
—An Iraq veteran from New Jersey

The United States has been fighting in Iraq for longer than it fought in World War II. Combined with the operation in Afghanistan, approximately 1.5 million U.S. troops have served in battle since 2001, 3,000 of whom have been killed in action—more Americans than were slain on our shores on September 11, 2001. [2] While medical and technological advances have helped save more lives in combat than in previous wars, the downside is that nearly 2,000 of those wounded in action suffer from traumatic brain injury, or TBI, usually resulting from this era's Molotov cocktail, the improvised explosive device.

In addition to the obvious physical injuries that many combat veterans carry home, an even greater number are being treated by the

Veterans Administration (VA) for crippling psychological injuries related to their wartime experiences.[3] The statistics are staggering: as of the end of 2006, one-in-four discharged Iraq and Afghanistan veterans (nearly 150,000) have filed disability claims, over 60,000 of which have been for mental health issues.[4]

But the grim numbers only tell part of the story. In August 2005, I came across an article in *Seattle Weekly* which made the plight of returning combat veterans come to life for me. "Home Front Casualties" covered what appeared to be a local issue, one that I had not heard much discussion of at the time:

> Altogether since 2003, there have been seven homicides and three suicides on Western Washington soil involving active troops or veterans of Iraq ... Five wives, a girlfriend, and one child have been slain; four other children have lost one or both parents to death or imprisonment. Three service members have committed suicide—two of them after killing their wife or girlfriend ... No one can say if the killing can be directly connected to the psychological effects of war. But most involve a risk factor distinctive to the military—armed men trained to kill—and some killers carry the invisible scars of war.[5]

One incident in particular hit a nerve: the story of Army Specialist Leslie Frederick Jr. At the age of twenty-three, Frederick had gone to Iraq, where he served fifteen months with distinction. Returning to Fort Lewis, Washington, he was among the first to receive the Army's new Combat Action Badge. Army Chief of Staff General Peter J. Schoomaker himself flew in to pin it on his uniform. Eleven days later, Frederick was found dead in his apartment, the victim of a self-inflicted gunshot wound. What had made this decorated soldier turn to suicide?

As I thought about Leslie Frederick, some questions started to circulate in my head:

- How could this have happened?
- Was this an isolated incident?
- What was our military and government doing to ease the problem?
- Why was there so little news of this in the public square?
- Why was our leadership silent on this issue?
- What could I do to help?

As I set out to learn more about the core issues facing our returning troops, I discovered post-traumatic stress disorder (PTSD). According to the National Center for PTSD, post-traumatic stress disorder "is a psychiatric disorder that can occur following the experience or witnessing of life-threatening events such as military combat, natural disasters, terrorist incidents, serious accidents, or violent personal assaults like rape."[6] In addition to the psychological symptoms, PTSD is marked by biological and physical changes, and often occurs in conjunction with other mental and physical problems, such as depression and substance abuse. The disorder is also associated with "impairment of the person's ability to function in social or family life, including occupational instability, marital problems and divorces, family discord, and difficulties in parenting." It is estimated that 30 percent of those who spend time in a war zone will develop PTSD.[7] And in today's theaters of war, where troops are dealing with extended and multiple deployments, twenty-four hour operations with no opportunity to unwind, sleep deprivation, ever-changing mission goals and guerilla warfare conditions where enemies and civilians blend together, it has been estimated that cases of PTSD may be higher than in past conflicts.[8] Already, nearly 40,000 soldiers have been officially diagnosed with post-traumatic stress disorder.[9] And those are only the ones that we officially know about—a 2004 study of Army and Marine troops returning from Iraq and Afghanistan stated that only 23 to 40 percent of those with PTSD actually sought treatment.[10]

However, despite the potentially catastrophic effects that PTSD is having on our returning combat troops and their families, not enough of us are paying attention to their plight. Three years after the invasion, a 2006 *National Geographic-Roper* poll showed that 60 percent of Americans were unable to point to Iraq on a map of the world.[11] Part of our lack of attention comes from sheer ignorance of what our troops are going through: while only 1 percent of the population has served in Iraq and Afghanistan, over 25 percent of America's men served overseas in World War II. Back then, the struggles of soldiers and their families were clearly visible through the lens of shared experience.[12] Today, most of us have not served, nor do we personally know anyone who has.

Despite our lack of personal familiarity, as Americans it is our responsibility to pay close attention to what happens to our troops after the parades and medal ceremonies are over. We need to honor our commitments to those who serve our country. My father, who was conscripted into the Hungarian Army as a young man, took up arms against the Soviets during the 1956 Hungarian Revolution and later served two years in the U.S. Army after having fled to America, is fond of saying, "You can always tell how a government feels about its people by looking at the way it treats its soldiers." Our government has continually lagged behind in providing the necessary resources to help treat our returning soldiers afflicted with PTSD. President Bush and the Republican Congress consistently underfunded the VA in the opening years of the war, while at the same time underestimating the number of service members who needed to apply for benefits.[13] This has led to inadequate funding and staffing at the VA, which in turn has caused unreasonable delays for veterans waiting to receive their healthcare.[14] A February 2006 report by the Veteran Administration's national advisory board on PTSD summed it up succinctly: "The VA cannot meet the ongoing needs of veterans of past deployments while also reaching out to new combat veterans of Iraq and Afghanistan and their families within current resources and current models of treatment."[15]

Despite all that was going on and all that needed to be done, other than the occasional news report, there wasn't much substantive or sustained media coverage of the issue of PTSD in our returning combat troops prior to 2006. That no one appeared to be cataloging the scattered incidents and shaping them into a narrative was surprising to me.

And so, with the nagging questions from the *Seattle Weekly* article compelling me to find the answers myself, in September 2005, I started collecting media reports of combat PTSD-related incidents. Eventually, my work developed into *ePluribus Media's PTSD Timeline*, a database designed to provide a starting point for further research, reporting and discussion of PTSD.[16] I also began writing my own articles to share what I had learned, and in February 2006, I started up my own online journal or blog, *PTSD Combat: Winning the War Within* (http://ptsdcombat.blogspot.com), to bring all of the information I had amassed together in one place. And now, nearly two years of writing and research has resulted in the book you hold in your hands, which I hope will become an all-in-one resource for the myriad health, social and political issues that our returning combat troops with PTSD face.

I do not profess to speak for our veterans. I do not "own" the war as they do. I am not a medical doctor or counselor. I am just an ordinary citizen who wanted to know how our troops were doing once they returned home. As a result, I have tried to reconstruct the experiences of some of our troops, in order to give ordinary citizens a glimpse of what the returning combat veteran has to go through as they transition from the battlefront to the home front.

Though it is filled with the narratives of war and its warriors, this book is really designed for the majority of Americans who will never journey to Afghanistan or Iraq. While most of us have not understood how desperately our soldiers and their families need our assistance, I do believe that most Americans have a strong desire to do right by those sent to war on their behalf. We want to help, but haven't been shown how.

Until now.

PART I—A BACKWARDS GLANCE

"I want to tell the story, not for the sake of telling it, but to try and change how things are perceived and maybe to alter the labeling."
—James Blake Miller, on combat-related PTSD[1]

1. THE FACE OF WAR

"This is going to come down to that young man, that 19, 20 year old corporal, lance corporal whether he's a soldier or a Marine, leading his particular fire team or his squad through the city, house by house, block by block, room by room."—Marine Major Francis Piccoli, *Voice of America*

Like John Wayne with smoke and fire trailing in his wake, Lance Corporal James Blake Miller rose out of the ashes of Fallujah on November 9, 2004.[1] Pushing through yet another building, Miller headed towards the roof along with his fellow Marines, sniper fire hot on their trail. Had it really been only two years since he had signed up for this? A lot of things can change in two years—a lot of things can change in two minutes in Iraq. Especially on the second day of the Battle for Fallujah.

Operation Phantom Fury (Operation al-Fajr, or "The Dawn" in Arabic) had kicked up in earnest the night of November 7, 2004. A week earlier, the British Black Watch Regiment had planted itself in the city's southwest corner to provide relief and protect the eastern flank once the invasion began. Power in the city was turned off, and residents were pelted with leaflets warning them to evacuate or face the fury of U.S. firepower. Air attacks that had begun in June were turned up another notch, pounding away at the city. These actions reduced Fallujah's population from approximately 300,000 to an estimated 50,000 to 75,000. Finally, a combat team had cordoned the city off, making it nearly impenetrable, as Iraq's Transitional Prime Minister Ayad Allawi declared a sixty-day state of emergency and round-the-clock curfew. All was now in place for the battle to begin.

The mission had two goals: to extinguish a seven-month-long rebel hotbed, and to allow the interim government to gain control of the chaotic metropolis ahead of the planned January 2005 national elections.

Well-trained and war-seasoned Army and Marine personnel mixed with members of other military branches for a combined ground and support force of 15,000. Another 3,000 freshly trained Iraqi forces covered the assault's rear, though their main purpose seemed to be for posed photo ops (such as after securing the Al Hydra Mosque).

Miller was a member of Charlie Company, 1st Platoon, which was part of the 1st Division, 8th Marines (1-8). The 1-8 was to barrel down the narrow urban streets and move south towards Highway 10. Swarming in from the north as part of a six-column formation known as a Regimental Combat Team, the 1-8 would drive a stake through the center of the city. Charlie Company was to cover the battalion's far-left flank.

At 1900 hours (7:00 p.m.), the 1-8 set in under a steady drizzle. Within three hours, they had advanced into the city's eastern Askari district, as tracers and rounds from tanks and planes lit up the besieged city. Once they reached the rim of Fallujah, however, all was quiet. The Marines were mystified until, in the dark mist, enemy rocket propelled grenades suddenly screamed down and engaged them, along with fire from unseen snipers.

Along with his fellow Marines, Lance Corporal Miller worked his way through the densely packed neighborhoods, the broken-up streets crackling under his feet, sniper fire whizzing by in the darkness. The city was a literal booby trap, improvised explosive devices planted throughout. As author Gary Livingston describes it in *Fallujah, With Honor*, the fight would take the Americans "down streets, into houses, room to room, floor to floor all the way up to the rooftop. Some houses would have underground tunnels and bunkers. It would be a fight to the finish."[2] One after another, structures fused to form a kind of cat-and-mouse maze. Each home or shop contained so many rooms with so many doorways. Prey slipped into one entryway and darted out another. Familiar with the layout, the insurgents had the clear advantage on the ground. For U.S. forces, getting up above the game and unto rooftops was vital.

And so, here they were. Twenty months after Operation Iraqi Freedom had been launched, Miller's squad found itself trying to hold their ground on the roof of a building as the rain stopped and a strong sun rose in the sky. Taking fire from just about every direction, they were so pumped that they almost shot Luis Sinco, their embedded *Los Angeles Times* photographer, as he dashed up behind them. "We had no idea he was coming up the stairs; in fact, we almost shot him," Miller would later say.[3]

It was a loud, hectic, and frantic engagement. Enemy fighters repeatedly rushed the building. Each time, Charlie Company beat them back. Eventually, however, the adrenalized war rush started to wear off, and physical and emotional exhaustion set in. No one had slept for nearly a day, and the last twelve hours had been spent in close combat with the nastiest opponents they had taken on since arriving in country.

Nerves were raw as Miller called in two tanks to end things once and for all, directing their fire towards the enemy, who happened to be holed up in the very building he and fellow Marines were standing on. Instantly, the section where the enemy had been was transformed into a smoldering pile of rubble. "You could feel your heart, like it was coming out of your chest," Miller would later recall, "It was insane." Later on, they would find nearly forty bodies in the rubble.[4]

During the battle, Sinco had taken cover behind a wall, and with the fighting over for now, Miller walked over to the photographer and sat down beside him, taking the weight off his back and feet for the first time since entering the city. The Marine grabbed a pack of cigarettes, methodically working his way through his five-pack-a-day habit. The two men didn't say a word to one another. "Man, this is amazing," Miller thought to himself, vaguely aware that Sinco was taking pictures. Drawing in the sun's rays along with the nicotine, Miller told himself that if he made it out of here alive, he would never take another sunrise for granted.[5] Trying to forget the world around him for a moment, the kid everyone called Smokey back home in Kentucky took another slow drag. "Man, here I am, 20 years old," he thought to himself. "I got my whole life ahead of me. I haven't done anything yet."[6]

A SHOT SEEN AROUND THE WORLD

On November 10, 2004, as Americans woke to learn the details of Operation Phantom Fury, over one hundred newspapers carried Sinco's photograph of Miller, cigarette dangling from his lips, his face covered in dirt and blood. News editors and television producers worldwide immediately connected to the image, one calling the figure staring back a "modern-day Robert Mitchum."[7] As daylight turned to dusk, *CBS Evening News* anchor Dan Rather introduced the Marine to even more Americans:

> "The picture. Did you see it? The best war photograph of recent years . . . It is this close-up of a U.S. Marine on the front lines of Fallujah. He is tired, dirty and bloodied, dragging on that cigarette, eyes narrowed and alert. Not

with a thousand-yard stare of a dazed infantryman so familiar to all who have seen combat firsthand, up close. No. This is a warrior with his eyes on the far horizon, scanning for danger. . . . See it, study it, absorb it. Think about it. Then take a deep breath of pride. And if your eyes don't dampen, you're a better man or woman than I."[8]

Encapsulating the perfect image of a valiant and virtuous warrior, the photo struck a cord. People christened the anonymous Marine the "Face of Fallujah." *CBS* went further, tagging him the "Face of War." Others just called him the Marlboro Man. Hundreds of letters and comments streamed into newsrooms across the country. One resident of Tallmadge, Ohio wrote the *Akron Beacon Journal*: "He is a young man and yet all the world weariness of someone at the end of a long, difficult life looks out at us from his eyes. He is tired, a down-to-the-bone type of exhaustion that the nicotine of a dozen cigarettes is not going to alleviate."

As the 1-8 continued to focus on subduing Fallujah's insurgency, Miller got wind that his picture was making waves back home. A gunnery sergeant told him at a briefing, "Would you believe you're the most famous fucking Marine in the Marine Corps right now? Believe it or not, your ugly mug just went all over the U.S."[9] When a *Los Angeles Times* reporter caught up with Miller two days after the photo was taken, the Marine said, "I just don't understand what all the fuss is about. I was just smokin' a cigarette and someone takes a picture and it all blows up."[10]

Fearing their famous Marine might get injured, Miller's superiors gave him the option of returning stateside. "I was like no way," he told them, "I came here with the guys that I am with, and some of them aren't even able to get back out of here."[11] Later, Miller recalled a visit from the commander of the 1st Marine Division, Major General Richard Natonski. "'You're a pretty famous Marine today,' Miller remembered Natonski saying. 'With all due respect, sir, I don't understand what's going on,' Miller replied. He said, 'Your picture is all over the United States right now. They were saying the picture would go into history books, and I thought that they were joking.'"[12] Even President Bush sent Miller a cigar and a congratulatory letter.[13] One battalion mate predicted: "Miller, when you get home you'll be a hero."[14]

"I ain't no hero. That is one thing I wish could be truly clarified," said Miller about all the attention. "I'm no more a hero than anyone over there. Every man, every woman that is not in the states, over there doing what they're doing . . . just to ensure that people here can enjoy their everyday life, and have the freedom they do. They're all heroes."[15]

THE SHATTERED IMAGE OF WAR

After his tour ended in January 2005, the media moved in to cover Miller's return stateside. *CBS Early Show* recorded his reunion with his mother. ("That's my son!" she had screamed in November 2004 at her TV when she first saw his image gazing back at her on the *CBS Evening News*). The next day, when he appeared on the *Early Show*, co-anchor Harry Smith asked Miller what it was like to be home. "It is truly unreal," he said.[16]

Miller now faced what every combat vet eventually faces—the adjustment from the battlefield to the home front. "For the most part, I mean, it was a big adjustment just trying to get in the mindset of being able to just roam, run around without fear of being shot at or where to look for danger," Miller said. "It's unexplainable . . . to go from that [combat zone] mindset to being able to walk around freely and just enjoy it."[17]

As winter drew to a close, the homecoming parties and television interviews tapered off. It was time to get back to living—whatever that was after Iraq. Miller was looking forward to building a life with his new wife, Jessica. Maybe open their own business and buy a house together. "Right now," said Miller, "I'm just glad I'm here."[18]

However, as time went on, he found himself unprepared to deal with his combat experience. "None of the Marines talked much about the strain that war puts on one's emotions," Miller said. "The 'wizards'—military psychologists—gave the returning troops a briefing on the subject, but nobody paid much attention."[19]

At first, Miller tried to ignore what was happening to him. When his wife told him he was tightening his arm around her neck in the night, he figured it would pass, as would the nightmares he was having about Iraq. However, one day, while visiting his wife at her college dorm, Miller had a flashback. Looking out the window, he thought he saw the body of an Iraqi sprawled out on the sidewalk. Eventually, Miller went to a military psychiatrist, who diagnosed him with post-traumatic stress disorder.[20]

When he should have been doing his healing, however, Mother Nature stepped in to rattle his progress. In August 2005, Hurricane Katrina roared into the Gulf Coast, and most of New Orleans found itself under twenty feet of water. The Coast Guard and other military branches were summoned to carry out search and rescue missions and secure the city. When his unit was called up for Katrina duty, Miller had to go, despite his PTSD diagnosis.

Wading through the flooded streets of New Orleans, Charlie Company's former radioman worried about flashing back to Fallujah's firefights and ambushes. Sadly, his worry came to fruition, as one day, Miller blacked out in a blind rage after a shipmate whistled the sound of a rocket propelled grenade. "Without even knowing what I'd done until after it was over, I snatched him up . . . slammed him against the bulkhead, the wall, and took him to the floor," he said. "I was on top of him."[21]

He was worried that he might do the same to Jessica. "If I was to act out, I don't know what I'd do," Miller says.[22] After seeing three separate military doctors, on November 10, 2005—exactly one year after his famous photo was splashed across the world—Miller was told his PTSD symptoms posed a threat to his fellow Marines, and he was given an honorable discharge from the service. "At first I was irate because I wanted to stay in and make a career out of it," he said. "I liked being a Marine . . . But . . . this is what I'm stuck with, so I've got to deal with it."

As 2006 opened, the media again ran photos of Miller—this time with the headline, "Marlboro Man has PTSD." "I want people to know that PTSD is not something people come down with because they're crazy," says Miller. "It's an anxiety disorder, where you've experienced something so traumatic that you were close to death."[23] He was far from the only one. In his platoon alone, Miller personally knew of five Marines who were coping with the same demons.[24] "The more and more I talk to (other guys), the more I found out there were a lot of Marines that are going through same or similar emotions," says Miller. "It's tough to deal with. Being in Iraq is something no one wants to talk about."[25] Some of them call him up and replay the horrors they witnessed and took part in on the streets and roofs of Fallujah. "A lot of people don't really see how the war can mess people up until they know someone with firsthand experience," says Miller. "I think people coming back wounded—or even just mentally injured after seeing what no human being should have to see—is going to open a lot of eyes."[26]

Miller has now become the chronicler of another war—the war within. Appealing to the country that declared him a hero because of a photograph, he asks to look beyond the image and see the human cost of war. "I want people to understand what PTSD is and what it can do to you—what it can do to your life."[27]

And this is where our journey really begins.

2. A BRIEF HISTORY OF PTSD

"There is a compelling reason to take a much wider look at what happened in the past: we are making a mess of this problem today and need to relearn the lesson that, in treating the aftermath of war, good intentions are not enough." —Ben Shephard, *A War of Nerves: Soldiers and Psychiatrists in the Twentieth Century* [1]

General George S. Patton, one of World War II's most controversial and successful Allied commanders, was well known for his brashness and brilliance. Yet, on his way to winning a hard-fought victory in the Sicily Campaign during the summer of 1943, a series of "slapping incidents" almost brought his stellar career to an end.

On the morning of August 3, 1943, Patton received word that General Dwight D. Eisenhower was awarding him the Distinguished Service Cross for "extraordinary heroism." [2] While touring the 15th Evacuation Hospital later that same day, Patton met an American private, Charles H. Kuhl, who did not appear to be seriously injured. When Patton asked the soldier what was wrong with him, Kuhl replied, "I guess I can't take it." Enraged, Patton slapped Kuhl's face with his glove, picked him up by the collar, and threw him out of the tent. [3]

Later that evening Patton grunted in his diary, "Companies should deal with such men, and if they shirk their duty, they should be tried and shot." Two days later, the general blasted off a memo to 7th Army commanders directing that, "Those who are not willing to fight will be tried by court-martial for cowardice in the face of the enemy."[4]

A week later, the general literally struck again while visiting the 93rd Evacuation Hospital. He spotted a shivering GI, artilleryman Paul G. Bennett, and inquired as to his condition. Bennett responded, "It's my nerves. I can't stand the shelling any more."[5] Patton barked back, "Your nerves, hell; you are just a Goddamned coward, you yellow son of a bitch. . . . You're going back to the frontlines and you may get shot and killed, but you're going to fight. If you don't, I'll stand you up against a wall and have a firing squad kill you on purpose." To be sure there was absolutely no misunderstanding it, he added, "In fact, I ought to shoot you myself, you Goddamned whimpering coward."[6] Patton then pulled his pistol from its holster and waved it in front of Bennett's face. After holstering the weapon, Patton proceeded to hit Bennett twice in the head with his fist, before the hospital commander intervened. Unknown to the general, Bennett had argued against removal from his unit, yet his battery surgeon had ordered his evacuation.[7]

When word of these incidents reached General Eisenhower, he realized the potential scandal that could arise, so he headed things off by demoting Patton, explaining, "No letter that I have been called upon to write in my military career has caused me the mental anguish of this one . . . but I assure you that [such] conduct . . . will not be tolerated in this theater no matter who the offender may be." Patton later said of his actions, "I was a damned fool."[8]

In the wake of the uproar, some wondered if Patton himself snapped due to his own combat stress. Private Kuhl, on the receiving end of the first outburst, suggested in the aftermath, "I think he was suffering from a little battle fatigue himself." Decades later a reporter conjectured, "Patton's difficulty was that he refused to acknowledge in himself the battle fatigue he deplored in his men."[9]

In his journal, Patton admitted having to turn away from one injured soldier "or I might develop personal feelings about sending men to battle. That would be fatal for a General." Handing out forty Purple Hearts the day before the first slapping incident, Patton confessed to an assembled crowd, "I do a lot of human things people don't give me credit for and I'm not as big a [expletive] as a lot of people think. The commander of invading troops is under great tension and may do things he later regrets."[10]

In truth, Patton was but one in a long line of soldiers affected by the strains of battle.

NOSTALGIA

Though it has been referred to by a number of different names, post-traumatic stress disorder has been with us for as long as wars have been fought. The Greek historian Herodotus, writing of the battle of Marathon in 490 BC, mentions an Athenian warrior who went blind when the soldier standing next to him was killed, although the blinded soldier "was wounded in no part of his body." Herodotus also wrote of the Spartan commander Leonidas, who, at the battle of Thermopylae Pass in 480 BC, dismissed his men from combat because he recognized they were mentally exhausted from previous battles.[11]

However, post-traumatic reactions were not exclusively reserved for those who fought in battle. Having survived the Great Fire of London in 1666, Samuel Pepys recorded in his diary the frightened, angry, and disturbed moods that haunted him for the next several months, even though he had been uninjured in the fire and his house undamaged.[12]

It wasn't until 1678 that a name was given to the symptoms

that made up post-traumatic stress, when Swiss physician Johannes Hofer coined the term "nostalgia." Initially called the "Swiss disease" because of its prevalence among Swiss men who fought in mercenary armies, nostalgia was characterized by "melancholy, incessant thinking of home, disturbed sleep or insomnia, weakness, loss of appetite, anxiety, cardiac palpitations, stupor, and fever."[13] Around the same time as Hofer's diagnosis, German, French and Spanish doctors noted similar symptoms in their combat troops.

During the Napoleonic era, French physicians developed a very advanced and modern understanding of the factors that lead to nostalgia, citing conditions ranging from the social to the environmental. Dominique Jean Larrey, Napoleon's chief surgeon, prescribed a course of treatment that, while biologically-based, took social factors heavily into account and was in many ways a precursor to our contemporary understanding of the psychiatric effects of warfare upon soldiers.[14]

THE CIVIL WAR

The American Civil War saw a significant rise in the number of soldiers who suffered from battle-related psychological trauma. During the war years, the Union Army recognized over 2,600 cases of insanity and 5,200 cases of nostalgia.[15] In addition to the official cases, many "insane" Union soldiers were simply discharged and left to find their own way home. The public outcry that resulted led to an 1864 War Department order requiring that such soldiers be transferred to the Government Hospital until their families could retrieve them.[16]

Desertion by psychologically traumatized soldiers was also a problem. Since those who were unable to fight were often singled out as "malingers" or "cowards," many soldiers deserted instead of being tagged with one of these labels. However, no matter which options a combat-stressed soldier chose, the penalty was brutal:

malingerers, cowards and deserters were executed by firing squad while their fellow soldiers were forced to watch. As a result, everyone clearly got the message of what happened to those who were unwilling to fight.[17]

In 1871, an internist named Jacob Mendez Da Costa wrote of the chest-thumping anxiety and breathlessness he had observed in many soldiers on the frontlines during his time as a Union doctor. The main symptoms of "the irritable heart of the soldier," or DaCosta's Syndrome as it came to be called, were a persistent tachycardia, or "hyper-arousal," which led to anxiety and hyperventilation.[18]

While Americans waged civil war, Great Britain was mired in an internal conflict of another kind. A number of deadly and highly publicized train accidents had rocked the nation, creating a trauma condition called "railway (or railroad) spine." First noted by an English surgeon in 1867, railway spine was "characterized by the manifestation of a variety of physical disorders in otherwise healthy and apparently uninjured railway accident victims." Attention to this new industrial age disorder spurred many in the medical profession to examine the role of psychological factors in "provoking" physical disorders.[19]

PSYCHOLOGY GOES TO THE FRONT

The first organized military system for psychological treatment of combat fatigue occurred during the Russo-Japanese War (1904–1906), when physicians were placed close to the front in order to perform evaluations of traumatized soldiers.[20] This system of "forward treatment" recognized the value of caring for psychological casualties as quickly and as close to the action as possible, as it was observed that the farther from the point of battle that a soldier traveled, the less successful doctors were in getting him back in the fight.

World War I ushered in a entirely new type of combat, as modern weaponry inflicted a brutal toll on the flesh and the mind. Captain F. C. Hitchcock, a British officer, reflected on this viciousness of this form of warfare:

> The noise . . . split our ears, and we all felt quite dazed by the brain-racking concussions. . . . A battery of French .75's . . . were so rapid that they sounded as if they came from some supernatural machine-gun. . . . The men of the Company were very bitter to think they had been shelled all day by an invisible foe.[21]

The "bitterness" that Captain Hitchcock wrote about reflected the violent circumstances of the modern battlefield, where the idea of fairness or control over one's destiny was blasted into oblivion by the magazine rifle, the machinegun and the quick firing artillery piece. As a result, a new term was adopted to describe psychologically traumatized soldiers: "shell shock." Soldiers who suffered from this condition literally acted as if they had sustained a shock to their central nervous system, often suffering from "staring eyes, violent tremors . . . and blue, cold extremities." In addition, many shell-shocked soldiers became deaf, blind or paralyzed, even though they were physically uninjured.[22]

To treat shell shock, British and French psychiatrists expanded on the work of their counterparts from the Russo-Japanese War, making forward treatment an integral part of the treatment process. In 1917, Thomas Salmon of the U.S. Army Surgeon General's office built upon the work of the British and French to create the first comprehensive treatment program for shell shock, or "war neuroses" as it was renamed. Salmon's system, which involved placing psychiatrists in combat units with forward hospitals to support them, centered around four key treatment principles, which remain the cornerstone for treating combat stress:

- Proximity (treating the soldier as close to the battle as possible)
- Immediacy (treating the soldier as soon as possible)
- Simplicity (providing simple treatment such as rest, a warm shower and food)
- Expectancy (the expectation that the solider will return to fight after he has been treated)[23]

Despite the progress made in the psychological treatment of traumatized soldiers during World War I, many of the conclusions that the medical profession reached turned out to be flawed. For example, they still clung to the notion that only the "weak" succumbed to wartime strain, as well as holding fast to the idea that rigorous pre-enlistment screening could help to separate those likely to experience shell shock and battle fatigue from those who could withstand the rigors of combat.

BATTLE FATIGUE

During the interwar years, the belief that pre-enlistment screening could minimize combat trauma cases became so prevalent that, when World War II began, psychiatrists were no longer assigned to combat divisions, and no provisions were made for psychiatric treatment in the field.[24] As a result, many of the successful "forward treatment" lessons of World War I were forgotten.

Unfortunately, the screening process turned out to be a complete failure. Despite the fact that twelve percent of the 15 million armed forces recruits during World War II were rejected due to psychiatric disorders (as compared to two percent during World War I), psychological casualties during World War II were 2.4 times greater than in World War I.[25] Not only was the screening process ineffective, it also hurting the war effort; by midway through the war, more soldiers were being kept out of the army than were being allowed to join.[26]

Despite the failure of the screening process, there were still important lessons learned about combat stress during World War II. One was that inexperienced troops were more likely to suffer breakdowns than seasoned soldiers. Another was that the threat of combat stress increased with the intensity of combat. Finally, and perhaps most importantly, it was learned that group morale was a contributing factor in preventing war trauma, as units with strong cohesion and leadership had fewer combat stress casualties.[27]

THE REAR ECHELON

The American military had still not corrected its deficiencies in treating combat stress when the Korean War began in 1950. As a result, initial trauma casualty rates were three times higher than during World War II. Rather than using the forward treatment techniques that had proven to be successful in earlier war efforts, psychological casualties were evacuated from the combat zone, greatly harming their chances at recovery. As Peter J. Murphy wrote in *Military Stress and Performance: The Australian Defence Force Experience*, "lessons in the management of both the psychological casualties of combat and returning veterans have had to be repeatedly relearned, at great personal cost to service personnel affected by the stress of war."[28]

Fortunately, due mostly to the efforts of Colonel Albert J. Glass, the principles of forward treatment were quickly reinstated, reducing the number of psychiatric casualities. Other procedures were also implemented in order to reduce combat trauma, including a rotation system for troops, and greater attempts to rest soldiers (rest and recreation or "R and R").[29]

Despite the overall success of combat psychiatry during the Korean War (approximately 90 percent of psychiatric casualties returned to battle), a new problem developed: the psychiatric problems of rear-area or rear-echelon troops. As the war progressed and support troops, who rarely found themselves in dangerous situations, came to outnumber those engaged in actual combat, psychological conditions similar to what had been seen in soldiers who had once suffered from nostalgia, including boredom and longing for home, became a problem. To seek relief from their symptoms, many rear-echelon troops turned to alcohol, drugs and sexual stimulation. Unfortunately, the problems of rear-echelon troops were for the most part ignored; they would go on to become the dominant psychiatric casualties of the next major U.S. conflict, the Vietnam War.[30]

POST-VIETNAM SYNDROME

"We don't promise you a rose garden."—1971 Marine Corps recruitment poster

Because of the Vietnam War's slow build-up, psychological casualties did not show up as quickly as they had in previous wars, and when they did appear, it was at a much lower level than in past conflicts. This was attributed to several factors, including the twelve-month rotation policy, the absence of sustained artillery fire and the lack of prolonged battles.[31]

It was in the aftermath of the war that the situation worsened, as veterans streamed into the Veterans Administration seeking help for trauma they were experiencing months and even years after their initial combat exposure. Dr. Matthew J. Friedman, who began a lengthy career with the VA in 1973, recalled how "People were flooding the clinics, demanding that we do something for their distress. We had no clinical terminology for what we were seeing. Their suffering was so raw."[32]

One of the main barriers to treating veteran's psychological symptoms was a lack of consistent terminology for their ailments, as there had been at least eighty different names for combat stress since the syndrome had first been recorded.[33] Much-needed relief from the cacophony of labels came when Dr. Robert Jay Lifton, a well-known research psychologist, used the term "post-Vietnam syndrome" at the Congressional Conference on War and National Responsibility in 1970. Dr. Lifton's use of the term in his testimony was literally a defining moment in the treatment of combat stress.[34] Partnering with Dr. Chaim F. Shatan, Lifton helped to add new focus and terminology to the combat psychology revolution. In 1980, their work, along with that of veterans, psychologists and anti-war activists, succeeded in convincing the American Psychiatric Association to add a definition for "Post-Traumatic Stress Disorder" to the third edition of the *Diagnostic and Statistical Manual of Mental Health Disorders* (DSM), the "Bible" of psychiatry.[35]

The DSM-I, published in 1950, had relied heavily on the input of World War II-era military psychiatrists for defining combat stress. Covering four pages, the definition stated that "gross stress reactions" stemmed from either catastrophes or combat. It also spoke of the "value of the stress definitions to military psychiatrists [and] psychiatrists working with veterans." But, ironically, all reference to such stress reactions was wiped completely from the DSM-II, published at the height of the Vietnam War in 1968.[36]

With the publication of DSM-III, the oversight was remedied. An official name and definition now in place, scientists and researchers were able to devote their energies to studying the *why's* of PTSD, and finally leave the *if* behind.

AFGHANISTAN AND IRAQ

The relative peacetime quiet in the decades after the Vietnam War meant that the issue of post-traumatic stress disorder largely faded from public view. However, things changed quickly in 2002 and 2003, as the nation became involved in Afghanistan and Iraq. And, just as they had done in World War II, military planners disregarded the lessons of forward treatment, to fatal consequences.

The first sign that something was wrong occurred in 2002, when there was a rash of murder-suicides at Fort Bragg. Four military wives were killed by their husbands, all recently returned Special Forces troops from Afghanistan. A year later, a wave of combat zone suicides in Iraq caused the Army to ask a team of doctors to determine whether the stress of combat and long deployments were contributing factors to their deaths.

As a result of all this, in 2004, the Army and Marines launched Operational Stress Control, embedding mental health personnel within deployed combat divisions. Greg Gordon, a spokesman for the Marine's Personal and Family Readiness Division, explained to a *Washington Post* reporter at the time that, "Before, we had to ship them out of the war theater. Now [the mental health professionals] can provide help immediately."[37] As of April 2006, more than 230 mental health practitioners were treating frontline troops for the emotional (sadness, worry, fear), cognitive (disorientation, confusion, memory loss, inattention), and behavioral (aggression, suicidal) components of combat stress disorder.[38] Mirroring the goals set forth in WWI, the overarching aim is to rapidly return the soldiers to duty. The hope is that early treatment will also reduce combat veteran's long-term mental health problems and its associated costs.[39]

THE EXPERIENCE OF TRAUMA AND PTSD

Trauma and disaster are part of the human experience. Statistically, 50 percent of us can expect to survive at least one traumatic event over the course of our lives.[40] As animals, we have a built-in ability to adapt to our changing environment, and to the stresses and circumstances of life. Our adaptability acts as protection. After a traumatic incident, it is natural to experience stress and preoccupation with the event. Though it may not feel "normal" at the time, replaying the episode is how our brain works to process, modify and integrate the stress before moving on.[41]

Unlike combat stress disorder, which is an immediate response to events taking place on the battlefield, post-traumatic stress disorder develops over time. Richard Pierce, a Vietnam veteran who has been a tireless advocate for returning combat veterans, describes the build-up of PTSD: "In its initial stages I think the nightmares, withdrawal, and anxiety are natural defensive reactions to a very traumatic experience. At this early stage it's like a tooth-ache, painful and troubling. Left untreated, the infection festers and grows. That's when it becomes an illness."[42]

PTSD leaves an unpleasant impression on the mind, like a scratch on an old vinyl record, which can cause permanent damage over time if left untreated. Dr. Edward Tick, a clinical psychotherapist with extensive experience treating veterans, refers to combat PTSD as "frozen war consciousness."[43] Time appears to stand still as the trauma survivor skips back repeatedly to the event through intrusive thoughts, nightmares, and other triggers. Each re-experience leaves the sufferer mentally and physically drained, and their anxiety and frustration increases as they continually feel out of control. Avoidance or rage may result, along with any number of other symptoms and reactions, such as:

- Depression
- Anger
- Alienation
- Jumpiness (startle response)
- Unrelenting "survival mode" stance
- Feeling of being "on guard"

- Feeling betrayed by God and/or society (cast off)
- Flashbacks
- Nightmares
- Survivor's guilt
- Cynicism
- Frustration
- Fear
- Negative self-image
- Problems with intimacy
- Distrust
- Irritability
- Poor concentration/memory
- Loneliness
- Suicidal feelings
- Preoccupation with thoughts of the enemy
- Revenge fantasies
- Addiction
- Alcoholism
- Feeling powerless
- Avoidance or numbing
- Resignation ("don't care")

With every trigger and re-experience, depressive emotional and biological patterns or habits are set down. Modern psychology calls these patterns neural grooves. Eventually, people coping with PTSD begin "organizing their lives around the trauma."[44] Their work, their family relationships and their long-term health usually suffer as a result.

It is important to note that being subjected to combat trauma does not automatically mean one will suffer from PTSD. Early intervention is key. Setting constructive and positive responses to triggers in their early stages increases the likelihood that the trauma reaction can be defused. Yet even with vigilance and all the right supports in place, the invisible scars of war can haunt a warrior for a lifetime.

On February 4, 2005, the Reverend Alan McLean, a Purple Heart and Bronze Star Vietnam veteran and popular rector at St. Luke's Episcopal Church in Wenatchee, Washington, composed a letter to his wife and kids on his laptop. In the message, he apologized to them for not being stronger, explaining that the war in Iraq had made his nightmares about Vietnam more powerful and painful. The former Marine second lieutenant added, "35 Marines died today in Iraq, [a loss] only slightly more noticed than my legs," referring to the strong limbs a landmine had taken from him thirty-eight years before.[45]

Initially, McLean had been supportive of the Iraq War, as he was of the war in Afghanistan, delivering a sermon on the need to have faith in the government's mission. Six months later, as the war reports extracted a heavy toll on his psyche, he delivered an opposing sermon to the small farming community that he ministered over. As flashbacks and panic attacks progressively destroyed what little peace he had managed to create for himself following Vietnam, on February 11, 2005, in his church office, he turned a pistol towards his chest and escaped the war-torn earth. His daughter would later say, "I underestimated the power of the war to take his life. And I really feel that, though my dad's been in Wenatchee, the war in Iraq killed him."

3. MARCH

"[O]ver time, soldiers develop a belief system (schema) about themselves, their role in the military, the military culture, etc. War can be traumatizing not only because of specific terrorizing or grotesque war-zone experiences but also due to dashed or painfully shattered expectations and beliefs about perceived coping capabilities, military identity, and so forth."
—The Department of Veterans Affairs Iraq War Clinician Guide

A LONELY APARTMENT

Exactly one year after Operation Iraqi Freedom claimed its first Marine casualty, on March 21, 2004, another would fall. Instead of on the battlefield, this drama unfolded in a quiet and lonely Renton, Washington apartment, nothing like the intense theater of war in which Corporal Ken Dennis was used to performing.

A 22-year-old who had arrived in Iraq with the initial invasion in 2003, Dennis was found dead in his bathtub by his best friend, an ordinary belt ending the life of an extraordinary individual. His father, Joe, remembered him as a "nine-year-old boy who was serious beyond his years," who ran to the closet at the start of the first Gulf War, "took out our flag and proclaimed that since we were at war, it was our duty as Americans to fly it."[1] His son would grow up to serve in Pakistan, Somalia, Djibouti and Afghanistan before finding himself in Iraq.

A Marine rifleman trained in special operations and antiterrorist missions, Dennis was part of the 15th Marine Expeditionary Unit (MEU) the day the terrorists struck the Twin Towers. At sea when the attack took place, Dennis was among the first to land on Afghan soil following a 400-mile helicopter flight to Camp Rhino in Kandahar. He put in thirty days of fighting before his brief tour ended.

Back in the states in January 2003, Dennis answered a call for troops with combat experience by joining the 11th MEU. As team leader in the 1st Platoon, Kilo Company, 3rd Battalion, he led his men through heavy combat in Nasiriyah and Baghdad. In six months, not one of his Marines lost their lives.

But just two months following the completion of his four-year enlistment and eight months after returning from the battlefields of Iraq, Ken Dennis was dead. Right before his suicide, he had confessed to his father, "You know, Dad, it's really hard—very, very hard—to see a man's face and kill him."

The same month that Dennis took his own life, Marine Private First Class Matthew G. Milczark, from Kettle River, Minnesota, joined him. On March 8, 2004, Milczark was found in a Kuwaiti chapel, dead of a self-inflicted gunshot wound to the head. Only eighteen years old, he had graduated from high school just ten months earlier. The former homecoming king was "a leader . . . one of those kids you would see in the hallway who automatically had that respect from others," said his school superintendent. "He was a good kid, happy-go-lucky and always smiling."[2]

One day after Milczark's suicide, twenty year-old Army Specialist Edward W. Brabazon's body was found in Baghdad, another apparent gunshot suicide. Based out of Fort Bragg, and hailing from Philadelphia, Brabazon had served in both Iraq and Afghanistan.

While home on leave during the Christmas holidays, he had visited the grave of his 9-year-old sister, who had died during his overseas tour. "He was so glad to be home," his mother said, "He didn't even want to go to Iraq, but he had no say."[3]

Two other non-combat fatalities were listed on March 2004's casualty rolls. Army Private First Class Bruce Miller, age twenty-three, was drawn to art, poetry and writing; he had joined the Army on his way towards fulfilling a dream of studying law. On March 22, he was found dead of a gunshot wound in Mosul, Iraq. His family described him as "a kind, thoughtful, and religious young man."

Three days after Miller's death, on March 25, 2004, Marine Lance Corporal James Casper, age twenty, was found dead in Al Asad, Iraq. He was on his second tour. Although Casper had joined the military to pay for college, he considered the needs of others more than his own. During his first tour, he had stayed behind to allow those who were married to get back to their families. He was also troubled by the condition of the Iraqi people. "Those people over there are just stuck. They can't work for it," his mother said, recalling her son's feelings. "That's what he was fighting for, the poor people in Iraq."[4]

Whether by suicide, accident or enemy fire, individuals who die while deployed are included in a war's casualty count. Future memorials will include their names. The nation they served will acknowledge their sacrifice and bravery. Stateside deaths, however, are not included in official casualty counts, even if they clearly stem from military service. The precise number of home front suicides that take place following combat deployment is unknown because the Defense Department does not collect that information. But, as documented in police reports, local newspapers and family memorials, home front suicides and other acts of violence after combat deployment frequently occur, and are on the rise.

A FOREIGN RAGE

In March 2004, the day before Milczark's body was found in a Kuwaiti chapel, Chief Warrant Officer William Howell killed himself in a frightening and uncontrollable rage. Based out of Fort Carson, Colorado, Howell had returned only three weeks earlier after serving ten months in Iraq. A thirty-six-year-old father of three, Howell was no disillusioned young soldier—he was a decorated seventeen-year Army Special Forces Green Beret.

Before coming home, Howell had filled out the required post-deployment evaluation forms and begun his demobilization processing, which includes PTSD screening and counseling, measures that were put in place following a cluster of post-combat murder-suicides at Fort Bragg in 2002.[5] Unfortunately, the new screening program is not bulletproof. Major Chad Storlie, a fellow Army Special Forces member and good friend of Howell's, is familiar with the forms used in the post-deployment debriefing process. They contain "probably six to eight" mental-health related questions: "Did you see any dead bodies? Are you having trouble sleeping? Have you thought of killing yourself or others? Fairly cursory."

In addition to the superficiality of the questions, military service members are also concerned about answering them truthfully, worried that they may lose a promotion, be kept from high-risk missions, be looked down upon or ostracized, or have homecoming delays if they admit to a problem during the "demob" process. Storlie punctuates these points, saying, "Rarely would someone mark [those kind of questions] on a record. Especially members of the Special Forces."[6]

In addition to reservations about answering honestly, Howell may have had another reason to keep his problems to himself: the case of Georg-Andreas Pogany. In October 2003, Pogany, an interrogator for the 10th Special Forces Group, the same unit that Howell served in, experienced intense physical reactions after seeing the effects of a machine gun on an Iraqi body. Looking to his superiors for help, they pushed down hard on him instead. Refusing to approve the care and rest prescribed by a military psychologist, they charged him with cowardice. Pogany thus became the first soldier since Vietnam to have to defend himself against such a charge—which is punishable by death.[7]

In addition to the case of Pogany, further evidence of the stigmatization, harassment and punishment of soldiers daring to come forward with psychological problems at Fort Carson was uncovered in two separate investigations in 2006—one conducted jointly by the *Colorado Springs Independent* and *CBS News*, the other by *National Public Radio*. *NPR's* extensive report led to calls from Senators Barbara Boxer, Christopher Bond and Barack Obama for a Department of Defense investigation into the matter.

But all of this came two and a half years late for Howell, whose life had begun spiraling out of control.[8] Now home with his wife and kids, the task of decompressing was left for him to deal with on his own. He initially drank to ease the transition. But his attempts at self-medicating failed, and on March 14, 2004, his war demons came on hot and quick as he struck his wife repeatedly during a fight that he had intentionally provoked. His wife, Laura, said later, "The guy standing in that door that night was not my husband. He in no way resembled him. The look in his eyes was, 'Who are you?' It was death."[9]

As her husband went to get his .357-caliber revolver, Laura grabbed the phone and called 911. After telling the operator that her husband had hit her and was going to get his gun, she hung up the phone and ran outside. When emergency services phoned the residence back, her husband answered and said everything was fine. Later, Laura was able to listen to the 911 tape. Of his voice, she said, "It was not him on the phone. It was empty . . . unemotional . . . ghost-like."

When the police arrived on the scene, Howell was chasing his wife around the yard. As the officers approached, the seasoned combat veteran took a revolver from his waistband and pointed it at his wife's face. "You are going to watch this. You are going to watch this," he said to her. Laura pushed his hand away, and a moment later, Howell put the gun to his head and shot himself.

What had happened to push this decorated war veteran, husband and father over the edge? While he was in Iraq, his Special Forces A-Team had been in the pressure-cooker of Samarra. He had lost one of his men to an improvised explosive device. A tough Sunni firefight led to the reported loss of civilian life. Did these events trigger the change in Howell's behavior?

In addition to these possible clues, his wife believes that Lariam, an anti-malaria drug developed by the Army (and considered a contributing factor in the 2002 Fort Bragg murder-suicides), may have had something to do with her husband's death, as he had taken it during his final deployment. The Army disagreed, however, saying that the drug does not cause one to become suicidal—which directly contradicts the Food and Drug Administration warning that "Lariam can cause panic attacks, thoughts of suicide, depression, anxiety, paranoia, delusions and psychosis that can occur long after taking the drug."[10]

"We need to deconstruct what made this person of character do what he did," Steve Robinson, Director of Government Relations for Veterans for America, told a *Denver Post* reporter. Don't hold your breath for that to happen. "The military," he said, "doesn't equate combat experience to suicide, crime, domestic abuse, or drug and alcohol abuse. They'll call it a civilian matter, case closed."[11]

Robinson, a Gulf War veteran, says we need to do better by our returning troops. "Compare the way we treat our soldiers with the way we treat an NFL quarterback," he says. "The quarterback twists his pinky, and he gets an MRI that day. We have veterans waiting months to get services at hospitals." Robinson calls this a "skewered sense of priorities." He adds, "We don't do everything we can to make our soldiers whole." As Dr. Gene Bolles, military regional medical center chief of neurosurgery in Landstuhl, Germany from 2001 to 2004 points out, "We have this [George] Patton image of soldiers. We don't want to hear that our soldiers can cry, that our soldiers are weak." But, as we've seen, even Patton succumbed to combat stress.

Looking back on her son's difficulties in adjusting to life after combat, Ken Dennis' mother said, "There should have been more one-on-one talks with other vets. There should have been more realizing that you just can't kick loose these young boys after what they've experienced and seen."[12]

INVESTIGATIONS

In the summer of 2003, a series of battle zone suicides and mental-health-related evacuations (6 percent of the 13,263 Army medical evacuations in the first year of the Iraq war were for psychiatric reasons) prompted Army Surgeon General Lieutenant General James B. Peake to form a Mental Health Advisory Team (MHAT).[13] Comprised of Army psychologists, psychiatrists and social workers, the assessment team arrived in the Middle East to interview those directly administering health care or making command decisions for the soldiers in the field.

In March 2004 (the same month the six men mentioned earlier in this chapter drew their final breaths) the findings were released to the public. Of the 756 soldiers interviewed by the MHAT, 52 percent reported low or very low personal morale, and 72 percent claimed their unit also suffered from the same confidence problems. However, the report refused to tie the morale problems to any of the mental health events that had occurred in the summer of 2003. In fact, the report pointed out that the Army suicide rate (17.3 per

100,000) was lower than the civilian rate for 18 to 34 year-olds (21.5 per 100,000).

Wayne Smith, a Vietnam Veterans of America Foundation spokesman, said at the time of the report's release, "We are concerned that the Army is equating the suicide rate in Iraq with that of the general population. This is misleading in the extreme, given that military personnel are supposed to be screened for the kind of psychiatric disturbances that can lead to suicide."[14]

On top of the morale problems cited in the study, the soldiers interviewed also said that they found it difficult to obtain psychological help when they reached out for it. Complicating matters, it was left to the individual to arrange armed convoys merely to see a doctor or go to the pharmacy.

The soldiers were not alone in their frustration. Battlefield mental health providers also reported several obstacles that were making their work more difficult, including a shortage of vehicles and radios to allow them to properly treat soldiers in the field, and a lack of proper medications. In addition, half of the providers had not received combat stress care training.

Reflecting all these troubles, the MHAT survey revealed that 75 percent of the troops in Iraq did not have faith in their immediate superiors, saying officers "showed little concern for their well-being." The survey also confirmed the stigma that was attached to any soldier who tried to use the mental health services that the Army provided for them.[15]

EXAMINATIONS

As the first anniversary of the Iraq invasion approached in March 2004, veterans' groups charged that the military was not abiding by its own laws when it came to gathering baseline pre-deployment medical information. Six months earlier, a September 2003 Government Accountability Office report had concluded that the

"Army and Air Force—the focus of the GAO's review—did not comply with the Department of Defense's force health protection and surveillance policies." Depending upon the base reviewed, 38 to 98 percent of required pre- and post-deployment health assessment questionnaires were missing from service member files. In addition, 45 percent of those on file had not been completed within the necessary time frame.[16]

On top of the questionnaire snafu, veterans groups pointed to another problem: sending troops into combat before having collected required pre-deployment blood samples. Such lapses, while seemingly trivial, make it difficult for a returning veteran to prove that they had been deployed in full health, which needlessly bogs down the already drawn-out VA medical claim approval process. Service members returning with combat-related health issues now had an additional headache to deal with.[17]

The ill winds of March 2004 kept blowing as the *Kansas City Star* reported that Guard and Reserve troops who didn't meet established medical fitness requirements were still being sent into combat. The newspaper obtained a copy of a memo written by the exasperated director of Germany's Landstuhl Army medical center. "Frankly," he complained, "we are burning out a lot of time and effort on shipping back folks who never should have come [to Iraq] in the first place." In response, a Pentagon official acknowledged that while some medically unqualified Reserve and Guard troops had been sent to Iraq, "the percentages [were] extremely small." At the time, there were about 120,000 troops in Iraq, 40 percent, or nearly 50,000, of which were National Guard and Reserve. Even if just 1 percent had been medically unfit, that would be 500 soldiers who were "likely to become patients at a military hospital."[18]

That same month, veterans groups protested a directive to scale back some components of the required post-deployment physicals after Brigadier General Richard Ursone, at the time the commander of the Army Medical Service Corps, said that the Army would discourage routine tests that might help detect combat-related health disorders. As a substitute, returning service members could opt to have the more time-consuming (but thorough) medical exam, or simply fill out a questionnaire called the Post-Deployment Health Assessment. Veterans' groups worried that this measure would result in a lack of detecton of future health problems, as they believed that most soldiers would opt for the PDHA questionnaire in the rush to get home as quickly as possible.[19]

"WE'RE THE FUTURE LEADERS OF AMERICA"

When America was attacked on September 11, 2001, Columbia's *Carolina Reporter* went to the University of South Carolina to record student's reactions to the devastation of the day. Among those they interviewed was Phillip Kent, just beginning his final year in the school's Reserve Officers' Training Corps program. Kent, who was looking forward to a career in the Army, was more familiar with the Middle East than many of his classmates, as during his freshman year he had written a research paper on the ancient Assyrian Empire. Although he could not have imagined it at the time, within two years he would be patrolling land that had once belonged to the Assyrians. "Ironically," his mother, Laura Kent noted, he was "assigned to provide security in Saddam Hussein's hometown of Tikrit—only a few dozen miles from the ancient capital of Ninevah."[20]

On this severe clear mid-September day, as he watched events unfold in New York City, Washington, D.C., and Pennsylvania, Kent told the *Reporter* that "America has been pierced by terrorist forces. If the Pentagon is on fire, you can bet there's going to be war." Leaning on his ROTC training, he added of his own role to come, "We're the future leaders of America, so it's our duty first and foremost to serve our country."[21]

2nd Lieutenant Phillip Kent arrived in Iraq in November 2003. It was autumn, fall colors dripping from the leaves that waved along the banks of the Tigris River. Fog often greeted morning risers, and an occasional downpour would flood the roads near the 411th company headquarters, where Kent served as a platoon leader with the 720th Military Police Battalion. Larger than all other Army MP battalions, the "Soldiers of the Gauntlet" were responsible for, among many other duties, "guarding enemy prisoners of war."[22] Kent's five months in Iraq would be spent assigned to Tikrit Prison.

Just before Kent's arrival, *The Wall Street Journal* had revealed details of an internal Army study that had "identified serious problems in military prisons in Iraq." The study noted that, "as of June 3, 2003, the Tikrit jail held 218 prisoners in facilities intended for 80." The report went on to state that there were no standard operating procedures in place for running the prison, and that the military police were "the division's 'fix-all' when it [came] to running the detention facility."[23]

As a result of these problems, the pressure on the MPs was enormous. Some pushed the stress inward, while others exploded. Two months before Kent's arrival, a prisoner named Obeed Hethere Radad had been killed by a guard who "shot [Radad] in the arm and abdomen with an M-16 rifle" after the detainee merely "leaned through concertina wire." The soldier was eventually charged with involuntary manslaughter.[24]

In addition to the prisoner situation, all eyes were on Tikrit for another reason: Saddam Hussein. Still in pursuit of Iraq's former dictator, American intelligence had put him in or near his birthplace of Tikrit. Preemptive arrests and searches were ongoing, and Kent's company aggressively carried out raids against Baath Party loyalists. The intensity at the tip of the Sunni Triangle ratcheted up with each arrest, each rumor, each Saddam sighting. Eventually, in December

2003, Saddam's former bodyguard, Muhammad Ibrahim Omar al-Musslit, was brought to the prison for high-pressure interrogation, where he cracked and gave up the deposed dictator's position.[25]

Three months later, in March 2004, Kent left Iraq. Happy as his mother was to lay eyes on her son upon his return home, she could not believe his condition. "I saw a shell of a man arrive in Fort Hood, Texas," Laura Kent remembers. "I hardly recognized him weighing only ninety pounds, dehydrated and depressed." Angry and struggling with feelings of guilt, Phillip felt detached from others and started using alcohol to dull his pain. Doctors also found him to be suffering from amoebic dysentery, a disease picked up from contaminated water that results in bloody diarrhea, cramps and fever.

Despite his condition, the Army placed him back on active duty. "Concerned and alarmed," his mother said, "I immediately sought the help of the Army's chaplain because Phillip was becoming more anxious, depressed, and had developed bulimia." He had also started talking about suicide. Finally, two months later, Kent was hospitalized for post-traumatic stress disorder. But he received just three days of hospital care. Soon after his release, "his behavior became irate," Laura Kent said. By November 2004, Kent's erratic behavior forced the Army to give him an early, but honorable discharge. Ever talented, patriotic and proud, the soldier's dreams now little resembled the ones he had had on that distant September day in 2001. "Phillip was a great asset to the corps' mission to liberate Iraq in support of Operation Iraqi Freedom," Laura Kent said. "After meritorious service in Iraq, returning home half a man and no aftercare. As a mother and a citizen I am outraged."[26]

Phillip Kent was only 26 years old when he took his own life on September 28, 2005. His name will never be listed on any future Iraq War memorials.

PART II—A GLIMPSE IN THE MIRROR

"When cultural protection and security fail, the individual's problems are proportional to the cultural disintegration. The avenues of vulnerability resulting from trauma follow the routes vacated by culture Paranoia substitutes for trust; aggression replaces nurturance and support; identity confusion or a negative identity substitutes for a positive identity."
—*Traumatic Stress: The Effects of Overwhelming Experience on Mind, Body, and Society*[1]

4. MEDIA, SOCIETY AND THE PACKAGING OF WAR

"I learned early that war forms its own culture. The rush of battle is a potent and often lethal addiction, for war is a drug, one I ingested for many years. It is peddled by mythmakers—historians, war correspondents, filmmakers, novelists, and the state. . . . War exposes the capacity for evil that lurks not far below the surface within all of us. And this is why for many war is so hard to discuss once it is over."—Chris Hedges, *War Is a Force That Give Us Meaning*[1]

THE REAL WORLD

As Bill McKibben wrote in *The Age of Missing Information*, Americans today "believe [they] live in the 'age of information,' that there has been an information 'explosion,' an information 'revolution.'" Part of this belief is based on the relative ease at which we can acquire information. Look how effortless it has been for us to watch news of the wars in Iraq and Afghanistan on television from the safety and comfort of our living rooms. But if our sense of today's world (and today's wars) comes from what is pulled through the flickering scenes on our television screens, we are in deep trouble. The TV world is not the real world. As McKibben noted, "we also live in a moment of deep ignorance

... An unenlightenment. An age of missing information."[2]

First, the good news. A June 2004 Pew Research poll revealed that a majority of Americans follow what is going on in the world around them. On an average day, 82 percent of us consume some sort of news (while down from 90 percent in 1994, this is still a pretty healthy percentage). Most of us spend approximately an hour each day catching up on the day's events, either by watching one of the 24-hour cable news channels, one of the network news shows, reading a newspaper or turning to the Internet.[3]

Problems become evident, however, when we drill down to the type of news we seek, and the quality and content of what we eventually find. Looking deeper into the statistics, we discover that only 31 percent of us consistently follow international news and politics, while 13 percent stay away from it altogether. Even as hundreds of thousands of our fellow Americans are deployed on a number of foreign fronts, the majority of us seem not to be interested in "hard" news coverage.

Not surprisingly, this lack of interest in serious news goes hand in hand with a general misinformation about world events. For example, in January 2003, two months before U.S. forces stormed Baghdad, *Knight Ridder* conducted a poll to gauge the nation's attitudes on going to war. While only one-third supported a unilateral, go-it-alone approach, approval of the war increased to 83 percent with two key caveats: the invasion had to be backed by the United Nations, and it had to be carried out by a multinational fighting force. Clearly, most Americans wanted the blessing of the international community before moving forward, and that war, should it come, not be the sole burden of the American military and taxpayer.[4]

Yet the poll also reflected some very serious misinformation on the part of the American public. For example, although two-thirds believed themselves to be well informed on the Iraq issue, 50 percent also believed that "one or more of the September 11 hijackers were

Iraqi citizens" when none in fact were.[5] Nevertheless, by the fall of 2003 (six months after our invasion of Iraq and coinciding with the second anniversary of the September 11 attacks), a Pew Research poll showed that the number of Americans who believed Saddam Hussein had something to do with 9/11 had jumped to 69 percent.[6] As late as September 2006, that number was still close to 50 percent.[7] An even more remarkable figure was revealed in a March 2006 Zogby poll, which showed that almost 90 percent of currently deployed American forces felt that the invasion of Iraq had been in retaliation for Hussein's role in the attacks of September 11.[8]

Why did such a large percentage of us believe—and continue to believe—this falsehood even though President Bush himself repeatedly (when pressed on the issue) admitted there was no direct connection between Iraq and 9/11?[9] The two key reasons were our media's failure to accurately inform us in the run-up to the invasion of Iraq, and our societal fear at facing the truth about the horrors of war.

MEET THE PRESS

"First, all successful democracies need freedom of speech, with a vibrant free press that informs the public, ensures transparency, and prevents authoritarian backsliding."
—President George W. Bush, May 2005[10]

In December 2006, Middle Tennessee State University's College of Mass Communication released the findings of a study that measured the attitudes of the American public towards the media. Of particular concern to the participants in the study were "media portrayals of the truth" in the form of one-sidedness (bias) or dishonesty (deception), or what Dr. Tom Cooper, one of the people behind the study, described as "issues orbiting truth-telling."[11] These findings, while troubling, showed that many Americans do in fact care about the quality and veracity of what the media reports.

Democracy and the press are strongly intertwined, as democratic systems cannot survive without a properly functioning free press. While we may have a love/hate relationship with the media, they still fulfill a vital role in government of, by and for the people. Because democracy relies on an engaged and informed citizenry for sustenance and direction, we need reliable and credible information to fuel the sober work of voting, self-government and, especially in times of conflict, waging warfare. War's gravity, cost and shared sacrifice demand an informed nation. Direct feedback on how our system is working, within the reasonable bounds of public disclosure and national security, is crucial for the proper functioning of our democracy. If our media fails to accurately report the news, or if we as citizens fail to pay attention to what is going on, then we cannot make the educated decisions necessary for us to do right by our troops, or ourselves, for that matter.

However, during the run-up to the invasion of Iraq, the American media failed to ask enough questions, or the right questions. There were several reasons for this. One was "access journalism," where those reporters who asked tough questions were denied access to top governmental sources. Another problem was the "bottom line" attitudes of most news organizations, where chasing profits, ratings and demographics is regarded as more important than reporting "hard" news stories. A third reason for the poor coverage was the fear of many reporters of being labeled unpatriotic if they asked unpopular questions.[12]

An additional factor that cannot be overlooked is the effect of media consolidation on news reporting. As large corporations and conglomerates gain control of more media outlets, severe limitations are being placed on the variety of information that is being offered, and "the lack of diversity that comes from [the] homogenization of opinions [is] completely antithetical to the creation of new knowledge."[13] The fewer voices that are allowed to speak, the less information we are able to compare, contrast and digest. This was revealed very clearly in the run-up to the invasion of Iraq, where most news organizations unquestioningly parroted the Bush administration's reasons for going to war.

Putting all these factors together, it is no surprise that the reporting in the run-up to the invasion of Iraq was less than accurate and informative. In hindsight, many news organizations have admitted dropping the ball concerning their pre-war reporting:

- As far back as 2002, Dan Rather admitted that, "We haven't lived up to our responsibility . . . We haven't been patriotic enough to ask the tough questions."[14]
- In a May 26, 2004 *New York Times* editorial, the paper admitted to finding "a number of instances of coverage that was not as rigorous as it should have been."[15]
- On August 12, 2004, the *Washington Post*'s Howard Kurtz reflected, "The *Post* published a number of pieces challenging the White House, but rarely on the front page. Some reporters who were lobbying for greater prominence for stories that questioned the administration's evidence complained to senior editors who, in the view of those reporters, were unenthusiastic about such pieces. The result was coverage that, despite flashes of groundbreaking reporting, in hindsight looks strikingly one-sided at times."[16]
- In June 2004, Peter Beinart, editor of the *New Republc*, wrote, "If the administration had been less duplicitous, we and others might have recognized that Saddam didn't have nuclear weapons . . . Maybe we were naive, but I didn't think they would lie to that extent."[17]

In addition to less than zealous reporting and investigating of the claims for war, voices that questioned the validity and truth of what the Bush administration were saying were often censored. An October 2002 article titled "Doubts," written by Thomas Ricks, a seasoned military reporter and author of the book *Fiasco: The American Military Adventure in Iraq*, revealed the reluctance of many military leaders to support the plan to invade Iraq. The editors of the *Washington Post* killed the story.[18]

And then there was the case of Phil Donohue. One month before the invasion of Iraq, MSNBC canceled Donohue's show, just as it had become the #1 ratings draw for the station, replacing it with *Countdown: Iraq*.[19] A leaked internal memo later revealed the reason for the cancellation: the liberal Donohue presented a "difficult public face for *NBC* in a time of war.... [Donohue] seems to delight in presenting guests who are anti-war, anti-Bush and skeptical of the administration's motives."[20]

One of the most grotesque examples of media censorship was the *Nightline*/Sinclair controversy. In 2004, *Nightline* presented "The Fallen," a program honoring those who had lost their lives in the Iraq War. Without the usual media bluster, flashy graphics or heroic war soundtrack, anchor Ted Koppel soberly read off the names of 721 soldiers who had been killed in action, while each service member's picture, military branch, rank and age appeared on screen.[21]

Instead of being celebrated, *Nightline*'s straightforward revealing of the faces of war met with a gale of disagreement from many quarters, particularly from the Sinclair Broadcasting Group, owner of over sixty television stations. Eight of Sinclair's *ABC* affiliates refused to air the show because it "appears to be motivated by a political agenda designed to undermine the efforts of the United States in Iraq [and] influence public opinion against the military action in Iraq."[22] While many protested, such as Senator John McCain, who wrote a letter to Sinclair's president and CEO saying, "Your decision to deny your viewers an opportunity to be reminded of war's terrible costs, in all their heartbreaking detail, is a gross disservice to the public, and to the men and women of the United States Armed Forces," Sinclair's actions brought out into the open the media's preference for keeping the realities of war hidden from the public.

This attitude has also been reflected in the government's ban on publishing the photos of the flag-draped coffins of service members who have been killed in action, which the media has followed almost without question.[23] While we are told that the ban is in effect to protect the privacy of military families, how does a near blackout of public memorials to our nation's fallen veterans protect those they left behind? If there were any time in history when the faces and voices of our returning veterans should be seen and heard, it should be during a time of war. President Bush himself agreed, in an October 2001 speech he gave to students at Maryland's Thomas Wootton High School. "In these difficult days here in America, I ask all of us, children and adults, to remember the valor and sacrifice of our veterans," he said. "Invite veterans to speak about their experiences in serving the country. . . . [They] show us the meaning of sacrifice and citizenship, and we should learn from them."[24]

THE WARRIOR MYTH

America is the entertainment capital of the world. As a society, our appetite for frivolous escapism is so powerful that it trumps nearly everything, particularly information about serious issues. As an example of our interest in entertainment over information, more Americans voted for an *American Idol* winner in 2006 (63.4 million) than voted for President Bush in the 2004 election (62 million).[25] This escapist attitude means that, instead of trying to find out the truth about what our combat veterans are going through, for many it is easier to put blind faith in the reliable myths of war that have long been perpetuated by television and the movies. As the veteran author Chris Hedges writes, "The myth of war is essential to justify the horrible sacrifices required in war, the destruction and the death of innocents. It can be formed only by denying the reality of war, by turning the lies, the manipulation, the inhumanness of war into the heroic ideal."[26] Other than the "Shock and Awe" coverage at the beginning of the invasion, we have seen very little actual coverage of the Iraq War on television, and little that is unpleasant or bloody. That is partially because of the media's refusal to show such images, and partially because of our own unwillingness to demand that they show it, as our comfortable, entertainment-driven lives all too often lead us to make the easy choice, and accept the media propaganda that war is a good thing and we are right to wage it.

PTSD challenges our notion of security, leaving society "resentful about having its illusions of safety and predictability ruffled by people who remind them of how fragile security can be."[27] To keep our illusions of safety intact, we have developed the myth of the heroic warrior, brave in battle, impervious to the psychological damage of warfare. John Crawford, a Florida National Guard veteran who served with the 3rd Battalion, 124th Infantry, wrote of this in his book, *The Last True Story I'll Ever Tell: An Accidental Soldier's Account of the War in Iraq*:

> War stories are told to those that have not experienced the worst in man. And to the listener's ears they can sound like glory and heroism. People mutter phrases like, "I don't know how you did it." And "I could never have done that." And they look at you wondering how you have changed, wondering if you have forever lost the moral dilemma associated with taking another person's life.[28]

We will often go to great lengths to maintain the façade of our war myths, even if it means bending the truth. For example, while Blake Miller was obviously a key player in the battle for Fallujah, in the book *Fallujah, With Honor*, a moment-by-moment account of the November 2004 retaking of the city, he is glaringly missing in action. Though the book is expertly reconstructed from news reports and Marine interviews, there is not a single mention of Miller, even though he was without a doubt the most celebrated figure in the armed forces at the time. An account of the battle through a heroic-colored lens, the book fails to capture the complexity of war and its private fallout, as Miller's postwar tale does not "fit" the typical epic narrative. Outspoken and open to a fault, suffering with PTSD, Miller no longer represents the mythic soldier. Yet his bluntness is the dose of reality we need in order to cure what ails us as a nation. Miller asks us to consider the costs of war for the individual rather than endlessly, and mindlessly, perpetuating the myths of gallant battles and Teflon warriors. Do we dishonor him and our other combat veterans by asking that they keep their more trying and painful moments hidden from view? Would we prefer that they subjugate their brutal war experiences to a glorified macho myth? Perhaps another way to ask the same question is to turn it on its head: Should Miller's PTSD take anything away from his accomplishments in uniform? Do his psychological wounds make his story any less compelling? Yet, with his disappearance in *Fallujah With Honor*, we may be witnessing the first round in the scrubbing of his story from the history books.

As Americans have become increasingly aware of the deteriorating situation in Iraq, more realistic coverage has finally splashed its way into the American news stream. Up until early 2006, the majority of guests booked on the most popular and influential political news shows were a laundry list of former generals, political pundits and government officials, most of whom were cheerleaders for the war. Rarely did we see the face of a recently returned combat veteran. Fortunately, the landscape has changed, and veterans like Paul Rieckhoff, founder of Iraq and Afghanistan Veterans of America and author of the best-selling book *Chasing Ghosts*, and Steve Robinson, Director of Government Relations for Veterans for America, are now front and center on our television screens, leading the charge to ensure that the voice of the returning soldier is heard.

However, in order for things to really change, we must be ready to listen to what our veterans have to say, and more importantly, accept the realities of war, and no longer hide behind the myths that we as a society have created to give ourselves the illusion of safety and security. We must change the channel, so to speak, and turn off the American idols so that we can embrace the real stories of our American heroes.

5. LEADERSHIP, POLITICS AND THE PRICE OF WAR

The Government's obligation is to help veterans overcome special, significant handicaps incurred as a consequence of their military service. The objective should be to return veterans as nearly as possible to the status they would have achieved had they not been in military service. . . . Particular emphasis should be placed on rehabilitating the service-disabled and maintaining them and their survivors in circumstances as favorable as those of the rest of the people. . . . War sacrifices should be distributed as equally as possible within our society. This is the basic function of our veterans' programs.
—A report on veterans' benefits in the United States, 84th Congress, 2nd session, May 9, 1956

Our leaders continually remind us that winning the "war on terror" is essential to our nation's future. In August 2006, Vice President Dick Cheney spoke to service members at Offutt Air Force Base in Omaha, Nebraska, saying, "The war on terror is a battle for the future of civilization."[1] On the fifth anniversary of the 9/11 terrorist attacks, in a rare address from the Oval Office, President Bush called the military campaigns in Iraq and Afghanistan, "the decisive ideological struggle of the 21st century, and the calling of our generation."[2]

Yet, if this is literally a fight for our way of life, why hasn't the average American been asked to do more? *New York Times* op-ed columnist Thomas L. Friedman reflected on this a mere year into the Iraq War:

> The message from the White House has been: "You all just go about your business of being Americans, pursuing happiness, spending your tax cuts, enjoying the Super Bowl halftime show, buying a new Hummer, and leave this war to our volunteer Army. No sacrifices required, no new taxes to pay for this long-term endeavor, and no need to reduce our gasoline consumption, even though doing so would help take money away from the forces of Islamist intolerance that are killing our soldiers. No, we are so rich and so strong and so right, we can win this war without anyone other than the armed forces paying any price or bearing any burden."[3]

More than four years into the war in Iraq, and nearly six into the war in Afghanistan, and those on the home front have not been asked to do anything out of ordinary, or give up anything extraordinary, for our soldiers in battle. And our troops are continuing to pay the price for our leadership's failure to bring all of America together in shared purpose and sacrifice.

GLORY DAYS

If ever there existed a time where sacrifice in the face of war was emphasized, it was during World War II. Tom Brokaw reflects on this era in his book, *The Greatest Generation*:

> They won the war; they saved the world. They came home to joyous and short-lived celebrations and immediately began the task of rebuilding their lives and the world they

wanted. . . . A grateful nation made it possible for more of them to attend college than any society had ever educated, anywhere. They gave the world new science, literature, art, industry, and economic strength unparalleled in the long curve of history."[4]

Even before the nation bequeathed its gratitude upon its returning warriors, it committed to the war cause by planting victory gardens, purchasing war bonds, rationing food, fuel, metal and rubber, giving blood and retrofitting industry to wartime production. Farming communities whose products were in need shuttered their schools so that students could pitch in at harvest time. "Rosie the Riveter" was the template for the women who worked in factories while their men were away fighting. To use that era's slang, personal sacrifice was "clearly the bomb."

The main force behind this movement toward personal sacrifice was the federal government, led by President Franklin D. Roosevelt, who in his famous "fireside chats" stressed that the war effort relied just as heavily on the actions of those on the home front as on those stationed at the frontlines. As Commander in Chief, Roosevelt called for "all hands on deck," and Americans responded in kind.

Unlike the visionaries of World War II, today's leaders seem averse to rousing us to play a part in the war effort. As a result, they have squandered the positive energy and unity that was prevalent in the nation after September 11th. Instead of being asked to sacrifice, we have been asked to keep shopping in order to feed our economy, to support the war no matter what the outcome or expense and to pay lip service to "support the troops" slogans while our elected officials slash funding for veterans' programs. The Bush Administration's public disengagement policy has destroyed any sense of national unity. As Eugene Jarecki, director of the film *Why We Fight*, deftly points out, "When you've lost national unity, the country has lost its most important line of defense. It's lost the willingness of its people to die for it."[5]

SERVICE AND SACRIFICE

In the days following the attacks of September 11th, 2001, President Bush received near unanimous support from a nation draped in red, white and blue. Megaphone in hand, he saw his job approval rating soar to a record 90 percent.[6] The Congressional partisan divide melted away when the Senate voted 98-0 and the House 420-1 to hand the president the power to wage war against those he deemed responsible for the attacks against our nation.[7] With a clear national mandate, on September 20th, 2001, the President addressed the American people, explaining what kind of sacrifice he would be asking of them:

> Americans are asking: What is expected of us? I ask you to live your lives, and hug your children. . . . I ask you to continue to support the victims of this tragedy with your contributions. . . . The thousands of FBI agents who are now at work in this investigation may need your cooperation, and I ask you to give it. . . . I ask for your patience, with the delays and inconveniences that may accompany tighter security. . . . I ask your continued participation and confidence in the American economy.

Exactly one month to the day of the attacks, the matter of sacrifice again surfaced in a prime time news conference:

> **Q:** Mr. President, I'm sure many Americans are wondering where all this will lead. And you've called upon the country to go back to business and to go back to normal. But you haven't called for any sacrifices from the American people.

The President: Well, you know, I think the American people are sacrificing now. I think they're waiting in airport lines longer than they've ever had before.[9]

The president's definition of sacrifice as enduring lines at the airport has continued to pop up in the years following 9/11. On August 29, 2006, NBC's Brian Williams asked the president: "The folks who say you should have asked for some sort of sacrifice from all of us after 9/11, do they have a case?" The President answered:

You know, we pay a lot of taxes. America sacrificed when they, you know, when the economy went into the tank. Americans sacrificed when, you know, air travel was disrupted. American taxpayers have paid a lot to help this nation recover. I think Americans have sacrificed.[10]

During World War II, citizens were asked to give up their material comforts and join together in a collective national effort for the good of their fellow citizens on the battlefield. During the current "war on terror," however, sacrifice has been defined as waiting in long airport lines and paying taxes.

ONE SOLDIER'S STORY

On March 25, 2003, *Army Times* photographer Warren Zinn focused his camera on medic Joseph Dwyer as he whisked an injured Iraqi boy to safety. After nearly ten straight hours of heavy overnight conflict with enemy forces near the village of Faysaliyah, the Americans had called for air strikes, and one bomb had hit a house, injuring the residents inside.[11] A snap of the camera and a stirring moment was frozen in time as Dwyer scooped up one of the injured, four-year-old Ali Sattar, and raced the scared and bleeding child to an area where he could be treated for his wounds.[12]

To those who saw the photograph on the cover of *USA Today*, it symbolized everything that was right about America. One reader wrote in to the paper to say that the photo "explains, as no words ever could, why so many Americans support this war." The writer also thanked the soldier "for being the American many of us aspire to become."[13]

Of his famous photo, Dwyer later commented, "To be honest . . . I was embarrassed by it. I saw so many heroic things like that." He confided to one reporter that, "It kind of made me stand out as the glory boy, but really it was one team, one fight."[14] Humble as Blake Miller, whose iconic image would later cause a similar stir, the medic was a hero to a nation grasping for signs that they were doing the right thing. And like Miller, Joseph Dwyer returned home from the war with PTSD.

Born into a family of police officers, Dwyer had enlisted in the army two days after 9/11. Based out of Fort Bliss, Texas, he was assigned to the 3rd Squadron, 7th Cavalry Regiment, 3rd Infantry Division, a scout unit described as "the tip of the tip of the spear." As the first line of attack, they pushed powerfully through Iraq, securing river crossings for the forces racing behind them to take the capitol. "It took 21 days to get to Baghdad," Dwyer remembered. "We had four days that we didn't get shot at."

The night before rescuing the young Iraqi boy, Dwyer's convoy had been ambushed by enemy fighters. As a rocket propelled grenade slammed into his Humvee, thoughts of his death, and how it would affect his wife and mother, swirled through his head. Twenty-four hours later, while the enemy was able to celebrate the ruin of three American Abrams tanks, Dwyer and his fellow soldiers had all survived the heavy fighting.[15]

Three months later, Dwyer was on his way home. He answered "no" to the standard post-deployment questions on witnessing or taking part in intense combat, explaining later that, "I wanted to go home, take a shower, hug my wife." Once he got home, however, Dwyer found himself feeling detached and fidgety, and struggled to perform the common, everyday tasks that we all take for granted. Once an extrovert, he now hated being out in noisy crowds. At restaurants, he always kept his eye on the door.

Things worsened as he wrecked a car trying to avoid an imagined roadside attack. Flashbacks haunted his days, nightmares his nights. Fearing Iraqis were tying to break into his apartment, he repeatedly locked out his pregnant wife. Soon, he was drinking heavily and sniffing inhalants. Desperately trying to regain control, he turned towards religion and tried to give up alcohol. However, no matter what he did, he found it harder and harder to reign in his demons.

Concerned friends tried an intervention, begging him to give up his weapons and get help. Dwyer refused. "I'm a soldier," he said. "I suck it up. That's our job." A few days after the attempted intercession, on October 7, 2005, deep in a delusional state, Dwyer was arrested after a three-hour standoff with police. Discharging "volley after volley" of gunfire in his apartment, he thought he was back in the sandstorm of Iraq. He had hit rock bottom.

Dionne Knapp, a former Fort Bliss medic who had been involved in Dwyer's intervention, said, "I'm angry because Joseph, when he came back from Iraq, he was a hero, and now when he needs help, nobody is helping him." She told the *El Paso Times*, "We gave [military and mental-health authorities] warning after warning after warning.... This could have been prevented." Another friend who took part in the intervention, Angela Barraza, added, "Joseph is the sweetest, most good-hearted man I've ever met in my life." She said that more needed to be done to help the man who had voluntarily taken her 3rd Division slot in Iraq in order to give her more time to spend with her new baby.[16]

With Dwyer's approval, his family and friends have come forward to speak about his fight with PTSD, hoping that his experience might inspire others to overcome the stigma against getting help. In an interview with a local TV station, Dwyer's older sister said of her brother, "To me he hasn't fully left Iraq." She added, "I want my brother back. . . . I want him to be healthy, I want him to have a life with his family and his pregnant wife and not [be] in pain, not hurting." She believes the U.S. military needs to do more for her brother—and for the rest of the returning combat veterans.[17]

BROTHER, CAN YOU SPARE A DIME?

On January 31, 2006, President Bush delivered the State of the Union Address, laying out his budget plans for the coming year:

> Keeping America competitive requires us to be good stewards of tax dollars. Every year of my presidency, we've reduced the growth of non-security discretionary spending. This year my budget will cut it again, and reduce or eliminate more than 140 programs that are performing poorly or not fulfilling essential priorities. By passing these reforms, we will save the American taxpayer another $14 billion next year, and stay on track to cut the deficit in half by 2009.[18]

In February, a few weeks after the address, the president's $2.77 trillion budget proposal for 2007 arrived. The Department of Veterans Affairs was allotted $80.6 billion, including $3.5 billion more in healthcare funds than in the previous year's budget. While that 11 percent increase looked good on paper, one-third of it, or $1.1 billion, was to come from "management efficiencies"—cash the VA was expected to find by cutting costs.[19] Never mind that the

VA's patient caseload had ballooned 22 percent from 2001 to 2004, or that veterans' medical costs had soared 69 percent since 2001.[20]

That same month, the Government Accountability Office presented a report to Congress that found that the "VA was unable to provide any support for the estimates in the President's past budget requests and that [the] VA lacked a methodology for even making the savings assumptions."[21] Unable to explain how it arrived at its efficiency projections, the VA told GAO investigators that they simply estimated "the cost associated with [the] VA's projected demand for health care services ... [with] the amount the president was willing to request."[22] Translation: the VA's estimates were shaped not by need, but rather by the amount the president was willing to dole out. The result of this potential $4 billion deception was that the VA was not adequately funded, "causing a decrease in veterans' access to the system, and a series of emergency supplemental budget requests in order to keep the system running."[23] Representative Lane Evans, Ranking Democratic Member of the House Veterans' Affairs Committee at the time, called it "Enron-styled accounting," adding, "Veterans needing health care are being penalized because of an accounting deception promulgated by this administration." Democratic Senator Daniel Akaka, ranking member of the Senate Veterans' Affairs Committee, added, "This Administration still does not count caring for veterans as part of the cost of war."[24]

Democrats were not the only ones outraged at the GAO findings. Thomas L. Bock, head of the American Legion (a traditionally conservative organization), was equally vehement, saying:

> The GAO report confirms what everyone has known all along. The VA's health-care budget has been built on false claims of "efficiency" savings, false actuarial assumptions and an inability to collect third-party reimbursements— money owed them. This budget model has turned our

veterans into beggars, forced to beg for the medical care they earned and, by law, deserve. These deceptions are especially unconscionable when American men and women are fighting in Iraq and Afghanistan.[25]

Here are a few examples of what an underfunded VA looks like:[26]

- Three operating rooms at the VA Medical Center in White River Junction, Vermont, were closed on June 27, 2005 because the heating, ventilation and air conditioning system had broken, and maintenance funds had been used to cover the budget shortfall rather than for the necessary repairs.
- In 2005, California's Palo Alto VA had more than 1,000 new patients waiting for a primary care appointment, one-third of whom had been waiting for more than three months. More than 5,000 had to wait over thirty days for a specialty care appointment; 1,400 had to wait for more than three months.
- Due to a budget shortfall, Florida's Bay Pines VA was forced to put veterans with a service-connected illness or disability rating of less than 50 percent on a waiting list. By mid-2005, 7,000 veterans had been waiting longer than 30 days for a primary care appointment.

LONG LINES AT THE VA

"VA therapists and counselors are dedicated, but VA's leadership is spreading them too thin. How can this increase in demand, coupled with the decrease in the frequency of care, not affect access and the quality of care VA gives veterans?"—Representative Michael Michaud, D-Maine[27]

While there are currently approximately 24 million veterans eligible for some form of VA healthcare benefits, a large percentage of them are not enrolled in the system. In 2005, for example, the VA provided preventative and primary health care to about 5 million veterans.[28] Dismayed at even this low rate of participation, some forward the notion that veterans' benefits are handouts and should be capped to plug the financial drain. Others, like veterans' advocate Larry Scott, disagree. He feels these costs are a part of waging war, maintaining, "Veterans benefits are like workmen's comp. You went to war. You were injured. Either your body or your mind was injured, and that prevents you from doing certain duties and you are compensated for that."[29]

The VA is the first line of defense in helping our injured and ill veterans. Its roughly 240,000 staff members, doctors, nurses, counselors and other professionals are dedicated to caring for veterans from the wars of the last century to the battles of today. In addition to medical and hospital services, the VA operates about 200 national Veterans Centers that supply a variety of support services for returning troops.[30] Due to the nature of war and its not-so-glorious aftermath, VA counselors perform some of the most exigent and draining mental health work imaginable. But as able and dedicated as these professionals are, they cannot do anything about the VA's budget problems, which translate into long appointment waits, frustrating claims forms, daunting claims processing periods and often, loss of benefits.

Trinette Johnson served in Iraq and returned home with PTSD that left her angry, forgetful and detached. Yet her disability claim took fourteen months for the VA to process. At the same time, they would routinely cancel her monthly counseling appointments. Though she benefited from initial care at Walter Reed Army Medical Center, she is disappointed with her current VA treatment. "I haven't been there in four months, and they haven't even noticed," she said in 2006.[31]

Too often, the problems at the VA lead to tragic results. Michael

Torok, a 23-year-old Army communications specialist, returned from Afghanistan suffering from PTSD that caused nightmares, a severe weight loss and an abrupt change in his personality. Not able to find work near Fort Bragg, where he had been stationed, he returned to his rural Illinois home. Two days later, he showed up for a VA hospital appointment to have a variety of deployment-related physical ailments checked. Doctors were not required at the time to determine if incoming patients had PTSD and thus did not realize that Torok was in trouble.[32] The day after his appointment, he told his parents he was going to visit a friend, but never arrived. Nineteen days later, on September 24, 2004, Torok was found dead in his car. He had stabbed himself once in the heart.[33]

Don Woodward served five months with the Army in Iraq. After his return home, he became withdrawn, dropped out of college after a semester, could not hold down a job and refused to seek counseling. After a suicide attempt, he agreed to finally obtain help through the VA. But with the system overwhelmed, the earliest opening for a mental health counselor was not for a month. In the interim, the VA prescribed him antidepressants. Woodward never made it to the counseling session, as his second suicide attempt was successful.[34]

In April 2006, the nation's leading military mental health experts convened at the 14th Annual National Tri-Service Combat Stress Conference at Camp Pendleton. The use, or overuse, of antidepressants and psychotropic drugs was a central topic of discussion. Bart Billings, co-founder of the conference, explained, "A doctor can see four or five patients an hour if all he or she does is write prescriptions [for drugs], which don't work about 50 percent of the time."

William Marshall, co-director of the conference and a VA primary care physician, confided, "I am concerned that we aren't cranking up the care for [the newest veterans'] needs. If we don't provide the necessary support, we could lose a large number of these veterans to homelessness, drugs and joblessness."[35]

WHAT'S PTSD GOT TO DO WITH IT?

> *"[T]he struggle for recognition of PTSD by its champions was profoundly political, and displays the full range of negotiation, coalition formation, strategizing, and struggle."*—Wilbur J. Scott, author of *Vietnam Veterans Since the War: The Politics of Ptsd, Agent Orange, and the National Memorial* [36]

On September 17th, 1945, Wyeth Pharmaceuticals ran an advertisement in *Life* magazine called "Three Lives Brightened by 'Deadly Nightshade.'" In the ad, a service member, just home from war, is seen hugging his son as his wife looks on lovingly. The copy reads:

> Sergeant Bob not long ago was suffering from what they call 'shellshock' in World War I. Today it's called 'battle reaction' or 'mental trauma.' Bad stuff. But Uncle Sam's doctors cured the Sergeant with modern psychiatric treatment–and the help of Deadly Nightshade.[37]

Although deadly nightshade, a plant that is used as an antidote to some poisons, wasn't really a cure for "battle reaction," the ad is interesting for several reasons. First, it presents shell shock or battle reaction as a normal, if trying, after effect of war. Second, the practice of psychiatry is treated with respect and admiration. Finally, the advertisement trumpets the benefits of an interdisciplinary treatment approach for combat stress, with medication and counseling working together to return the soldier to full health.

Sixty years later, that post-World War II sophistication has lost its sheen. We now have a government that is more interested in spending money on armaments than on veterans, and a society that is unenthusiastic about looking at the psychological wounds of warfare. This cause and effect relationship of a secretive government and an ignorant public has created a battle between those who advocate on behalf of soldiers suffering from PTSD, and those who believe that those who try to call attention to the plight of our returning combat veterans have gone too far in their advocacy. Ben Shephard describes this tug-of-war in *A War of Nerves: Soldiers and Psychiatrists in the Twentieth Century*:

> Some see this train of events as a triumph, a 'self-help success story,' in which 'informed public opinion prevailed' and a group of victims fought for their rights. To others, it is a tragedy, a disastrous incursion of politics into medicine, the hijacking of traditional values by a small minority of activists, the elevation of the pathological into the mainstream.[38]

Rather than try to help those with PTSD, some would rather pretend that it is not a significant problem, or that it doesn't exist at all. In a 1985 *Associated Press* piece trumpeting Ohio's Brecksville VA Hospital, the only one in the nation at the time that offered a fully funded, comprehensive PTSD program, hospital director Jack Smith disclosed:

> There are VA people who think PTSD is a bunch of hogwash. The reason we don't want to recognize PTSD is that we as a country, the armed forces and VA, have always operated under the assumption that normal people don't have any psychological reactions to warfare.[39]

Another reason that some try to repress PTSD advocacy is because, as a VA official told the *Washington Post* in 2005, "If we show that PTSD is prevalent and severe, that becomes one more little reason we should stop waging war." However, if the general public is kept in the dark about PTSD and its effects upon on our troops, "that is convenient for the Bush administration," and others in the government who are determined to keep the war machine in Iraq and Afghanistan going.[40]

HIDING IT

The silence of our leaders on the issue of PTSD has left most Americans unaware that the VA has predicted "a surge in disability claims and appeals that are expected to send disability and survivor entitlements soaring by more than 81 percent in 2007 over 2000 levels, an increase of $15.4 billion." And this is not just a short-term increase, as the VA predicts that "these payments will hit $59 billion in 2016, up from $34.3 billion in 2007."[41]

One particularly insidious way that the VA tried to rein in costs was by challenging the official diagnosis of PTSD. In August 2005, the VA announced plans to review the claims of 72,000 veterans who were already drawing full PTSD disability benefits, with an eye toward rejecting some of them. While precious time would be devoted to reviewing previously approved cases, a backlog of 582,204 VA compensation and pension claims would simmer on the backburner.[42] While many worried that the review would adversely affect veterans coping with debilitating PTSD symptoms, as well as delay help for soldiers who were in desperate need, others, like University of Oklahoma sociology professor Wilbur Scott, disagreed. He felt that a review was in order, saying at the time that, "PTSD went from being problematic, to being accepted as a condition, to being almost too easily accepted."[43]

While a public backlash forced the VA to back away from its

plan to review the old cases, they were able to eliminate one case just by making a public announcement of their intent. On October 8, 2005, Greg Morris was found dead in his New Mexico home, a folder of articles outlining the VA's plans to review old PTSD cases, his Purple Heart and a gun by his side. His elected representative, Tom Udall, had received inquiries from Morris before his suicide concerning the upcoming review. "He believed, as so many veterans do, that he was being forced to prove himself yet again," Udall said. "It is that belief that makes veterans so angry and so frustrated with this process."[44]

Despite being forced to drop the planned review, the VA found yet another way to try and challenge previously approved PTSD cases, this time by questioning the very definition of PTSD. In February 2006, the VA contracted the Institute of Medicine to "review the scientific and medical literature related to the diagnosis and assessment of PTSD, and to review PTSD treatments (including psychotherapy and pharmacotherapy) and their efficacy."[45] Completing its review in June, the IOM advised the VA to continue using the definition for PTSD found in the *Diagnostic and Statistical Manual of Mental Health Disorders*. In addition, the chair of the IOM group announced that, "The committee strongly concludes that the best way to determine whether a person is suffering from PTSD is with a thorough, face-to-face interview by a health professional trained in diagnosing psychiatric disorders."[46] While the VA has now been stopped on two separate occasions in its attempts to cut veterans who were receiving PTSD benefits from its rolls, it is only a matter of time before they try something new to deal with their budget shortfall. And they will eventually succeed if the public is not vigilant.

DERIDING IT

On top of the VA's continuing attempts to deny PTSD benefits to those already receiving them, another problem that soldiers with combat stress face is resistance from the military itself when they come forward with PTSD-related symptoms. In the summer of 2006, *CBS News* investigated the complaints of nearly a dozen Fort Carson soldiers who had asserted that "their cries for mental health either went unanswered or [that] they found themselves subject to unrelenting abuse and ridicule" from their superior officers after they complained of classic PTSD symptoms such as nightmares, flashbacks and anxiety attacks. In addition, a local psychologist told investigators that she was treating twenty-five "emotionally broken" soldiers because they were too afraid to ask for help on the base.[47]

One soldier, Private Ryan Lockwood, who had returned from a yearlong tour in Iraq in August 2005 with a Combat Infantry Badge and PTSD, said that a superior officer had "threatened that if I tried to get a medical disability for my PTSD, he would make my life a living hell." In turmoil, Lockwood began drinking heavily. Eventually ordered to complete a two-hour substance abuse treatment program, he attended but received no additional counseling to deal with his nightmares and other symptoms of PTSD. In the end, instead of offering assistance, the Army began discharge proceedings against Lockwood. "They cast me out," he says. "I was having problems with day-to-day duties, so they just decided to get rid of me, despite my service to this country."

As the IOM met to begin their study of the definition of PTSD for the VA in February 2006, a hard-hitting three-part series published by ePluribus Media entitled *Blaming the Veteran: The Politics of Post-Traumatic Stress Disorder* stated that the Lockwood incident and others like it amounted to a virtual "swift-boating of the American veteran." Those who try and shove combat PTSD, and its moral lessons and financial costs, into the closet "trumpet the view that the source of PTSD resides solely within the individual and not with the war itself. The soldiers hailed as heroic upon deployment find themselves, upon their return, portrayed as [having been] psychologically impaired *before* they went to war, morally weak, or untruthful, malingering veterans." Gulf War veteran and advocate Kirt P. Love, who has testified extensively before Congress on PTSD-related issues, says that the "DOD/VA still use the old trick of patronizing a person into walking away . . . soldiers are taught 'tough guy medicine' and they don't want to complain because they look weak, which is very much to the DOD's advantage."[48] Retired Naval Commander Jeff Huber adds, "As a former military officer, nothing makes me sicker about the current state of affairs than treating soldiers as disposable items."[49]

Because of the wall of resistance that the military puts up when troops with combat stress try to obtain help, many soldiers have no choice but to self-medicate with drugs and alcohol to treat their PTSD. Yet, when these same soldiers are caught taking illicit substances, they are forced out of the military with other-than-honorable discharges, which prevents them from their receiving VA benefits.[50]

Army specialists Patrick Doherty and Dwayne Turner are two soldiers who learned how harsh the military is on those who try to tame their PTSD with drugs and alcohol. Doherty served in Iraq from May 2003 to July 2004 as a combat medic with Headquarters Company, 1st Battalion, 35th Armored Regiment, 1st Armored Division. Based out of Wiesbaden, Germany, the 1-35 was the first armored division to see combat during World War II. Yet during Doherty's tour, the historical lessons of limited deployments coupled with adequate rest and relaxation were disregarded.[51]

Most of Doherty's time in the Iraq Theater was spent patrolling "Sniper Alley" (Baghdad's Haifa Street). During his tour, he witnessed the death of friends, treated wounded soldiers and Iraqi civilians, and cleaned up bloody streets after suicide bombs had been set off. Despite the intensity of his environment, over the course of his fifteen-month deployment (his initial twelve-month tour had been extended an additional three months to contain the Moqtada Al-Sadr uprising in April 2004), he received only one four-day break at the Green Zone's "Freedom Rest" compound.

When Doherty left Iraq, he completed the standard post-deployment screening forms. During the process, the battalion surgeon checked the box for "REFERRAL INDICATED FOR: Combat/Operational Stress Reaction"; a psychologist noted he had "Mental Health Symptoms/risk factors;" and a physician recommended "Urgent consults (before block leave)" for mental health. Yet even with all of these recommendations, most of them unknown to Doherty at the time, there was no follow-up, no attempt to check up on him when he returned to garrison life.

Visiting his parents in Boston on leave in August 2004, Doherty was angry, telling his father, "We are just killers, the Army is just a bunch of killers." Once back in Germany, Doherty requested an assignment to one of the German medical clinics that he was due to be rotated to at the end of the year. Instead, he was slated to be sent to Fort Bragg for possible rotation right back to Iraq. As his father describes it, that is when he "slipped off the rails." By the end of the month, Doherty had tested positive for marijuana. "I was given no hope, help, or treatment by my chain of command," he says. "I got into more trouble with marijuana. I was not given any treatment, and was told I was going to be thrown out of the Army with a bad discharge."

Despite three years of service, fifteen months in combat, being awarded the Army Commendation Medal and a Combat Medic Badge, receiving Letters and Certificates of Achievement and a promotion to Specialist 4, Doherty was given an other-than-honorable-discharge. "I feel the Army took advantage of my combat stress condition to strip me of all my benefits," Doherty says in the wake of all he has been through. "I served well in Iraq and risked my life on many occasions, and I think I could have been rehabilitated if I was given some treatment and a second chance."

Unfortunately, Patrick Doherty's situation is not unique. Fellow Army medic Dwayne Turner served in Iraq with Fort Campbell, Kentucky's 101st Airborne Division, earning a Purple Heart and Silver Star for saving the lives of two of his fellow soldiers when their unit came under attack. That feat made him the most highly decorated soldier in his division at the time.[52]

Like Doherty, however, Turner returned from combat burdened by his wartime experiences. Diagnosed with acute stress disorder, as well as PTSD, he kept his flashbacks and nightmares at bay by binge drinking. He considered suicide, slashing his wrist one evening before quickly treating the wound. Finally buckling under the pressure of trying to keep his life together, and even though his medical discharge paperwork was pending, Turner went absent without leave. Two days later, he returned to the base, where his required urinalysis tested positive for marijuana. Rather than rehabilitation, the Army booted him out with a general discharge, which is the least serious form of discharge (though he lost his college reimbursement). Some believed that his Silver Star medal was the only thing that shielded him from a more punitive discharge. Whatever the case, Turner admits, "I can't run away from my problems, I need to face it." His sense of personal responsibility made him return after going AWOL, and still guides him today. But he contends, "They don't understand. They think you're pretty much supposed to be normal when you come back from war, and I don't understand that."[53]

Doherty's father, Thomas, a twenty-five year military veteran, is outraged at the unjust treatment his son and others have received following exemplary service to their country. "There are probably hundreds of Iraq and Afghanistan veterans who are being kicked out this way. Not only do they suffer from PTSD, they now have a bad discharge and no benefits." He says that at least forty combat veterans have been other-than-honorably discharged for marijuana use in his son's unit alone. "I am very angry about this, it's a big injustice," he argues. "They could have punished and [then] rehabilitated these soldiers . . . but it appears they are trying to save money by abusing [them]."*

BLEEDING IT DRY

Since September 11, 2001, the United States has spent nearly half a trillion dollars on the wars in Afghanistan and Iraq. Adjusted for inflation, that total equals nearly the entire cost of the Vietnam War. We are spending approximately $18,000 a minute in Afghanistan and $100,000 a minute in Iraq, or $7,800,000 an hour, and $169,920,000 per day, for both wars combined.[54] While the lives of the PTSD-encumbered veteran and their families are shattered by the human cost of the war, the taxpayer bears the financial burden. And the costs are piling up. In September 2004, Steve Robinson, Director of Veternas Affairs for Veterans for America, in conjunction with the Center for American Progress, published a paper called *Hidden Toll of the War in Iraq: Mental Health and the Military*, in which he wrote about the potential long-term costs of PTSD on the American economy:

> If a 24-year-old married male soldier with one child were to develop PTSD to the degree of unemployability, that soldier could receive compensation payments from the VA of over $2,400 per month for the remainder of his life.

---

* In October 2003, the Israeli Army agreed to a study conducted by Jerusalem's Hebrew University involving the use of the active ingredient in marijuana, Delta-9 tetrohydrocannabinol, or THC, on a group of its soldiers returning from the Palestinian front. The lead researcher, Raphael Mechoulam, asserted at the time, "It helps them sleep better, for one thing. These people often wake up from nightmares, and experience sweating or hallucinations."

Over an average male lifespan, such costs could amount to more than $1.3 million, not counting inflation.[55]

The enormity of the "PTSD problem" in our returning combat troops threatens to undercut not only returning veterans' treatment and care, but the nation's future financial priorities as well. A January 2006 paper, *The Economic Costs of the Iraq War: An Appraisal Three Years After the Beginning of Conflict*, by Linda Bilmes and Nobel Prize-winning economist Joseph E. Stiglitz, calculates that American taxpayers can expect to cough up at least $2.3 billion annually to cover the costs of caring for disabled Iraq and Afghanistan veterans. This figure is in addition to the $2 billion already being paid out annually to 169,000 veterans of the first Gulf War.[56] Added up, the outlay for caring for disabled veterans from these three conflicts will set the United States back $4.3 billion a year.

Like the first Gulf War, the invasions of Afghanistan and Iraq were marketed as relatively short and painless wars of precision and swift victory. That rosy scenario, quite like the promised flowers awaiting our forces, hasn't materialized. If any hope did exist that first summer following the invasion, by now it has been crushed under into a civil war's violence, with our troops caught in the middle.

6. THE RUMSFELD REVOLUTION IN MILITARY AFFAIRS

"Power is increasingly defined, not by mass or size, but by mobility and swiftness. Influence is measured in information, safety is gained in stealth, and force is projected on the long arc of precision-guided weapons. This revolution perfectly matches the strengths of our country—the skill of our people and the superiority of our technology. The best way to keep the peace is to redefine war on our terms."—George W. Bush, September 23, 1999[1]

HUBRIS

In a campaign speech delivered at the Citadel on September 23, 1999, presidential candidate George W. Bush outlined the powers he would grant his secretary of defense, should he become Commander in Chief. Whoever Bush appointed would receive "a broad mandate—to challenge the status quo and envision a new architecture of American defense for decades to come."[2] Seven years later, on November 6, 2006, the man selected by Bush to oversee this new type of military ("faster, lighter, more lethal") sent out the last in a long line of his infamous communiqués. In a confidential memo addressed to the White House, Secretary of Defense Donald Rumsfeld admitted for the first time that the strategy in Iraq was not working and that a course correction was necessary. "In my view it is time for a major adjustment," Rumsfeld wrote, adding that, "[c]learly, what U.S. forces are currently doing in Iraq is not working well enough or fast enough."[3]

The admission that all was not well in Iraq was at jarring odds with Rumsfeld's past jousts over the media's use of terms like "guerilla war," "counterinsurgency," and "civil war" to describe the unraveling situation in Iraq. "Recast the U.S. military mission and the U.S. goals," Rumsfeld wrote in the memo, suggesting that the Bush administration wage a campaign to lower the American people's expectations of what victory in Iraq would look like. "Announce that whatever new approach the U.S. decides on, the U.S. is doing so on a trial basis. This will give us the ability to readjust and move to another course, if necessary, and therefore not 'lose.'"[4]

Whether the memo was written for political purposes or reflected a genuine change of heart, it was nevertheless a breathtaking turn for a man who had long resisted any change to his Iraq policy. Instead of reacting to the situation on the ground, Rumsfeld had spent much of the war "arguing powerfully for his mistaken point of view," a point of view that was always dangerously optimistic. British defense expert Andrew Rathmell spoke of this "optimism" back in 2005: "This unwillingness to challenge assumptions and question established plans persisted during the course of the occupation, giving rise to the ironic refrain among disgruntled coalition planners that optimism is not a plan."[5]

In reality, war is immensely unpredictable, and can rarely be controlled by those who wage it. As Andrew J. Bacevich wrote in *The New American Militarism: How Americans Are Seduced by War*, "[s]ince the beginning of the industrial age, war has time and again proven itself to be all but ungovernable."[6] Rumsfeld's Achilles Heel was that he failed to prepare for, or react to, the unwanted outcomes and unexpected setbacks of warfare. The root of many of these problems can be traced to the massive restructuring that Rumsfeld put the military through, which Army Chief of Staff General Peter J. Schoomaker described in 2004 as the "most important and controversial reorganization in decades," one that would "affect virtually every soldier in the service."[7] Bacevich sketched out Rumsfeld's general vision of how the new military would look in *The New American Militarism*:

> ... General Tommy Franks initially conceived of the global war on terror as a series of Desert Storms—large scale, deliberately planned offensives permitting the United States to bring to bear overwhelming force. This prospect did not find favor with Secretary Rumsfeld and his top civilian advisers, who advocated a bolder approach, one that placed less emphasis on large mechanized formations and greater emphasis on air power supported by special operations troops, and lighter, more agile ground forces. The general offered plodding orthodoxy; the defense secretary wanted novelty and dash.[8]

Rumsfeld's ideas for "novelty and dash" were based largely upon the work of Andrew Marshall, a longtime government defense official who developed a philosophy of warfare know as the "Revolution in Military Affairs," or RMA. Believing that traditional ideas of warfare were no longer relevant in the modern, lightning-fast information age, the RMA advocated changing the military from a large, slow-moving force into something that was "lean, nimble and, above all, 'smart.'"[9] In this new model, protecting "one's own information systems and being able to degrade, destroy or disrupt the functioning of the opponent's information systems," should be America's chief military goal.[10] When Rumsfeld was named Defense Secretary in 2001, he immediately tried to implement the ideas of the RMA. However, he made little headway until after 9/11, when President Bush's declaration of a global war on terror, with its corresponding nontraditional battlefield methods, allowed Rumsfeld to put Marshall's ideas into action.

Unfortunately, half a decade of warfare in Afghanistan and Iraq, "which was supposed to prove the operational effectiveness of the new RMA and to set the U.S. military on the path of 'transformation,'" has instead shown the severe limitations of the philosophies of the RMA.[11] Instead of the quick victories that were predicted back in 2002 and 2003, we find ourselves involved in a Vietnam-like guerrilla war. However, as things deteriorated in Iraq, rather than trying to chart a new course, Rumsfeld continued advocating for his failed strategy. As reporter and author Thomas Ricks wrote, "[Rumsfeld] was focused on transforming the military, seemingly unaware that history almost certainly will judge him largely on his mishandling of the Iraq war."[12] Retired four-star commander and decorated Vietnam veteran, Army General Barry McCaffrey was even harsher in his assesment, saying that "[Rumsfeld's] legacy will be one of bad judgment and arrogance that has put this country in a position of great strategic peril . . . as things started to go badly, Rumsfeld and his team went from arrogance to denial, disingenuousness, and finally blatant lying about the state of things in Iraq and inside the U.S. military."[13]

MORAL FAILURE

In the end, Rumsfeld's greatest failure was not one of strategy but of morality, as he neglected the most important responsibility given to a defense secretary, that of properly protecting and supplying the troops in his care. The list of Rumsfeld's mistakes in this area is endless: inadequate body armor for soldiers in combat; overtaxed troops serving extended and multiple deployments; the use of

National Guard and Reserve forces as fully activated combat troops; ignoring the advice of his generals as to adequate troop levels. Rumsfeld's strategic misjudgments and subsequent unwillingness to change course have left our combat troops without the necessary physical and emotional tools that they need to successfully fight a war. Jonathan Shay, noted author and VA psychiatrist, says that there are three "supports" that the military is obligated to provide for its combat troops, none of which is adequately provided by the new military model that was championed by Rumsfeld:

1. In-depth and realistic training in what they will face in battle, and the proper equipment to do their job
2. Unit community and stability (cohesion)
3. Capable, moral, and reinforced leadership

The name that Shays gives to these supports is "thémis," Greek for "what's right." He says that the lack of these supports can trigger combat stress. "Military psychiatrists have been telling us at least since World War I that these three things can prevent some (not all) of the life-long symptoms that can follow prolonged heavy combat."[14] During his tenure, Rumsfeld continually failed to do "what's right" for our combat troops, and the consequences of his actions have had a detrimental effect not only on the physical and psychological well being of our soldiers, but on our military's capabilities as a fighting force. As Frederick Kagan of the conservative Enterprise Institute said, "When Rumsfeld took office, a lot of us cheered that here was someone who was going to take control of the U.S. military and help transform it. But you have to say that because of a number of bad judgments, the force Rumsfeld is handing off to Secretary Gates is de facto much weaker than the one he inherited."[15]

CONSEQUENCES

> *"We did not ask our soldiers to invade France in 1944 with the same armor they trained on in 1941. Why are we asking our soldiers and Marines to use the same armor we found was insufficient in 2003? The failure to provide the best equipment is a serious moral failure on the part of our leadership."*
>
> —Col. Thomas X. Hammes, U.S. Marine Corps (retired)[16]

Sergeant Perry Jefferies was awarded both the Bronze Star and the Legion of Merit during his twenty years of service in the United States Army. During the initial invasion of Iraq in March 2003, he served with the 4th Infantry ("Iron Horse") Division, sharing responsibility for over 400 troops and more than a hundred vehicles as they made their way over the fiery sands of the Sunni Triangle. History will remember the 4th ID for capturing Saddam Hussein on December 13, 2003.[17]

Previously an instructor at the U.S. Army Armor School in Fort Knox, an experienced veteran like Jefferies was in an ideal position to judge the effectiveness of the "new" military that Donald Rumsfeld had put into place. His judgements were not positive. "We are told that we have to be 'weaned' off of bottled water," he wrote in a letter home, "since we have only 2 of our 4 water trailers … this will be interesting." In addition to the water shortage, his unit also lacked basic hygienic necessities, like showers and bathrooms, and each soldier was limited to two MRE's (Meal Ready to Eat) per day. Furthermore, supplies like oil and spare parts were in short supply. "I watched America provide doors, floors, windows, plumbing, sewage disposal, and air conditioning for Iraqi troops while American soldiers on the same compound struggled with none of these things," Jefferies, now retired, remembers. "It wouldn't be right to keep convicts like this but it's okay in the Rumsfeld Army."[18]

Jefferies' anger at the lack of basic military supports has been echoed by many other service members. On December 8, 2004, during a Q & A session with Secretary Rumsfeld in Kuwait, Specialist Thomas Wilson of the Tennessee National Guard mustered the courage to stand and voice a concern that was weighing on everyone's mind. "We're digging pieces of rusted scrap metal and compromised ballistic glass that has already been shot up, dropped, busted—picking the best out of this scrap to put on our vehicles to go into combat," he said. "We do not have proper armament vehicles to carry with us north."

Rumsfeld looked into the sea of sand-brown uniforms before him. "As you know, you go to war with the army you have, not the army you might want or wish to have at a later time," he shot back. Reloading, he added, "You can have all the armor in the world on a tank, and a tank can be blown up. And you can have an up-armored Humvee, and it can be blown up."[19]

FATAL CONSEQUENCES

The longest continuously serving regiment in the United States Army, the 2nd Armored Cavalry Regiment deployed to Iraq in March of 2003. Known as the "Dragoons," the 2nd ACR's job was to provide reconnaissance and security for the 1st Armored Division. Sweeping out on patrols during the opening months of the invasion, the cavalrymen of the 2nd ACR conducted cordon and search operations, in the process arresting former regime elements and confiscating weapons. They also shut down a counterfeit dinar-printing operation.[20] Among their members was 20-year-old Specialist Leslie Frederick Jr. from St. Joseph, Missouri.

Though not trained to be an urban peacekeeping force, the regiment did its best to adapt, repairing war-damaged roads and sewers, building schools, and delivering humanitarian packages of food, clothing and toys. Yet, no matter the efforts on their part, the pace of the insurgency continued to quicken. On August 19, 2003, eastern Baghdad's Canal Hotel complex, which housed the headquarters of the United Nations, was bombed. Twenty people lost their lives, another seventy were injured, and the shock wave blasted in the 2nd ACR's windowpanes a half mile away.[21] In October, Sadr City's Baliyda Government Building was taken over by Moqtadr al-Sadr's forces. The 2nd ACR rode in and recaptured it. Later that month, the "Ramadan Offensive" kicked off with a mortar attack on the Abu Ghraib police station, as emboldened insurgents targeted the newly trained Iraqi forces and high-value targets like the Rasheed Hotel, where the Coalition Provisional Authority was headquartered. On the second day of the sacred Muslim observance, four more Baghdad police stations and the offices of the International Committee of the Red Cross were rocketed. Within two weeks, countless Iraqis were dead, along with sixty U.S. troops. One Special Forces soldier said it "felt like the whole city was blowing up."[22]

Like Perry Jefferies' 4th ID on the Iran-Iraq border, the 2nd ACR operated a training school, the Iraqi Civil Defense Corps Academy at Camp Muleskinner. By February 2004, 1,500 forces had been graduated, which gained the attention of Secretary Rumsfeld. The mood was high as he swooped in by helicopter on February 24 to tour the facility, stand for photos with the troops and pass out his official commemorative coins. "I am so proud of you all for what you are doing for your country," the Secretary said. "The future of Iraq is in your hands."[23] Two weeks later, when 116 noncommissioned officers, the "backbone" of the ICDC, graduated from the academy, there was a sense of accomplishment and closure.[24]

Like the rest of his fellow soldiers, Leslie Frederick looked forward to the end of his twelve-month tour and his return home. However, as the day of striking tents neared, Moqtadr al-Sadr's group, the Mahdi militia, still had not been fully contained. As a result, on April 8, 2004, Frederick and the entire 1st Armored Division got word that their tours were to be extended by three months. Paul Rieckhoff describes the feelings that soldiers experience when their tours of duty are extended:

> I have never seen so many grown men cry as when an extension was announced in Iraq. Extensions crush morale. Especially for Guardsmen and Reservists. My unit was extended at least four times. . . . Jobs are pushed back, birthdays are canceled, academic semesters are missed, marriages are ended, kids are crushed. Families back home take it especially hard. They are planning their lives around their soldier or Marine coming home around a certain time. They prepare everything around that time. Then it is yanked out from under them. It is unnecessary, even cruel. It damages the forces, encourages people to leave the military, and ultimately creates a weaker national defense.[25]

Heading south to Najaf and Karbala to measure swords with Sheik al-Sadr's militia, Frederick and his fellow cavalrymen were forced to retrofit their skills yet again as wide-open spaces replaced the compact city streets they were used to patrolling.[26] Finally, after several months of fighting, al-Sadr agreed to disband his militia. For its work, the 2nd ACR earned two Presidential Citations. Frederick, who was wounded, received a Purple Heart and a Bronze Star. On a sweltering July 4, 2004, *CNN Sunday Morning* covered the close of the cavalry's notable tour by taping their "casing of colors" (flag folding) ceremony at Baghdad's airport. Frederick was on his way home at last.[27]

However, after fifteen months of constant adjustments while in Iraq, upon their return home, the members of the 2nd ACR found out that they would face even more adjustments, courtesy of Donald Rumsfeld's military reorganization. The unit was to be transformed into a Stryker Brigade Combat Team, its base of operations shifting from Fort Polk, Louisiana, to Fort Lewis, Washington. Since radical change of this kind increases stress, the Army committed to "taking care of its soldiers during this time of transition." The move got underway for the 3,900 soldiers and their 11,000 family members during the winter of 2004-2005.[28]

As a result of the transition, it would be at Fort Lewis, not Fort Polk, that Leslie Frederick Jr. would stand before Army Chief of Staff Peter J. Schoomaker on July 15, 2005 to receive the newly created Combat Action Badge. The award recognizes those who engage or are engaged by the enemy during combat operations. Schoomaker, himself a former 2nd ACR squadron executive officer, told the twelve soldiers who were honored that day, "I can't tell you how proud I am of this Army and these soldiers." A week earlier, pinning the first handful of badges on troops in Washington, D.C., Schoomaker said of those receiving the commendation, "They represent our Army, the total Army, all the way across them, every piece of them." Of the decoration, he added, "The Combat Action Badge will go down in history as a very, very esteemed representation of the Warrior Ethos, of what being a soldier and a warrior stands for."[29]

Though this accomplishment must have been a source of great pride, the Iraq War and the effects of Donald Rumsfeld's subsequent military realignment had brought change, and the resulting stress, to every facet of Frederick's life. While every solider is susceptible to breaking under these kinds of pressures, Frederick was especially vulnerable; estranged from his wife and child in the wake of his 15-month deployment, his divorce became final the week after his decoration ceremony. Four days later, on July 26, 2005, Frederick lifted a gun to his head, putting an end to a short but distinguished life and career. A family member stated at the time that the "stress of having to kill while in battle really got to him."[30] Buried with full honors, Fort Leavenworth's Military Honors Detail playing Taps and firing off a 21-gun salute, his aunt Glenda Wilson, tears in her eyes, called her nephew a hero.[31] Another hero lost to the pressures of coping with warfare, exacerbated by the stress of dealing with the shortcomings of Rumsfeld's new military.

First published in the *U.S. Cavalry Manual* in 1923, "Fiddler's Green" is an anonymously penned ballad that describes the mystic place where cavalrymen go after they are killed in action. It is still used today to memorialize the deceased.

Fiddler's Green

Halfway down the trail to Hell,
In a shady meadow green
Are the Souls of all dead troopers camped,
Near a good old-time canteen.
And this eternal resting place
Is known as Fiddlers' Green.

Marching past, straight through to Hell
The Infantry are seen.
Accompanied by the Engineers,
Artillery and Marines,
For none but the shades of Cavalrymen
Dismount at Fiddlers' Green.

Though some go curving down the trail
To seek a warmer scene.
No trooper ever gets to Hell

Ere he's emptied his canteen.
And so rides back to drink again
With friends at Fiddlers' Green.

And so when man and horse go down
Beneath a saber keen,
Or in a roaring charge of fierce melee
You stop a bullet clean,
And the hostiles come to get your scalp,
Just empty your canteen,
And put your pistol to your head
And go to Fiddlers' Green.

7. 21ST CENTURY WARFARE AND PTSD

"No matter how the business of war is adorned by parades, uniforms, and literary glorification of the warrior's courage, and however it is burdened by administration and logistics, the soldier's real work is in killing. The soldier's privilege to kill is unlike anything most other individuals have ever experienced, and the soldier who kills is permanently changed, fixed to the death he has made."—Theodore Nadelson, M.D., author of *Trained to Kill: Soldiers at War*[1]

Staff Sergeant Zack Bazzi, who served a year in Iraq with the 3rd Battalion, 172nd Mountain Infantry Regiment, believes that today's military is a fighting force unlike any other in American history. "There's a fundamental difference between the modern day current military and previous militaries," he says. "Our current military is a professional, volunteer army. People go in there and get indoctrinated in the training and it's something they do for a living." Bazzi, star of the award-winning documentary *The War Tapes*, explains that while those who fought in previous wars were no less heroic than today's soldiers, "there's a difference between our army and theirs."[2] The difference that Bazzi speaks about results from today's training techniques, which attempt to turn our fighting men and women into Rambo-like killing machines.

Prior to the abolition of the draft in 1973, the military was comprised mainly of ordinary citizens who were drafted to fight in a specific war, with the assumption that they would return to their civilian lives once that war was over. Instead of creating soldiers who will fight, but will later have the ability to return to normal life, today's training concentrates on creating professional soldiers whose job is to kill, with little worry about how this kind of training will affect them once they return home.

To desensitize its recruits from the emotions associated with killing, today's military uses the latest advances in science, psychology and technology. The U.S. Army, for example, uses a program called "Total Control," and an April 2006 exposé in *Rolling Stone* revealed the success of this program: "The Army turns out 20,000 infantrymen a year; no other institution in history has trained so many to kill so effectively in such a short time. The number of soldiers who fail to return fire has fallen from seventy-five percent to nearly zero."[3]

Before they can be shaped into lethal instruments of war, recruits must overcome what author Dave Grossman calls "the universal human phobia," the aversion that most people have to committing aggressive acts against others. In his book, *On Killing: The Psychological Cost of Learning to Kill in War and Society*, Grossman forwards that "there is within most men an intense resistance to killing their fellow man. A resistance so strong that, in many circumstances, soldiers on the battlefield will die before they can overcome it."[4] Since World War II, studies have shown that only about 2 percent of the military population has a "natural-born killer" tendency, yet this 2 percent "typically accounts for up to 50 percent of the killing by a unit."[5] The rest need to be conditioned into pulling the trigger. As Blake Miller has said about the job of killing, "It's one thing to be shot at, and you shoot a couple rounds back, just trying to suppress somebody else. It's another thing when you see a human being. Knowing that you're shooting back with the intent to kill them. You're looking through a scope at somebody, [and you] can make out the guy's eyes." He added, "In order to do your job in combat, you have to lock up your emotions. Basically you're turning people into killers."[6]

The tools used by the modern American military to achieve their overwhelming kill rates are increasingly sophisticated and cunning. Informed by data generated by The Army Research Institute for the Behavioral and Social Sciences, the military trains recruits to unlock the psychological safeties that most of us have in place against using lethal force. As a consequence, a soldier walks out of basic training conditioned to "accept a moral obligation to kill."[7] A sampling of the techniques used in this effort include:

- Conducting killing exercises in realistic environments by using virtual reality video games like Battlezone and Doom. (The non-military version was a favorite of the Columbine High School killers.)[8]
- Teaching soldiers how vulnerable they are to being killed if they do not act by making repeated references to IEDs, mortar fire, tripwires, etc.
- Conditioning soldiers to hyper-bond with their M-16 ("That's your life right there. When I don't have it, I feel naked.")[9]
- Firing target practice until the action is reflexive and not reflective. Recruits pull the trigger over 2,000 times before the tenth week of basic training
- Strong reward/punishment feedback that conditions recruits to strive for success and fear failure

While these training techniques make today's soldiers the most effective killing force in history, they are ineffective in preventing soldiers from the long-term psychological harm that comes with being so good at killing. Former West Point philosophy instructor Army Major Peter Kilner says that, "[c]onditioning soldiers to reflexively engage targets prepares them to deal with the enemy, but it does not prepare them to deal with their own consciences."[10] Kilner was sent to Iraq in 2003, where he found that, unlike in previous wars, most infantrymen had "looked down the barrel and shot at people, and many [had] killed."[11] This increased exposure to killing translates into a higher level of post combat trauma. "Many combat soldiers experience feelings of guilt in the months and years following their wartime actions," explains Kilner. "[They] killed the enemy when their nation and its leaders have asked them to do so, only to later suffer guilt."[12] Dr. Rachel MacNair, Director of the Institute for Integrated Social Analysis, an organization that performs research on violence-related issues, has studied the effect of killing on Vietnam veterans, and found that soldiers who had killed in combat—or believed they had—suffered higher rates of PTSD.[13]

To mitigate their feelings of guilt, Kilner believes that troops should be taught from basic training on that they do have a justified reason for killing during wartime: self-defense. "It is morally permissible to kill another person under certain conditions: that another person has consciously decided to threaten your life or liberty, that that person is imminently executing that threat, and that you have no other reasonable way to avoid the threat." Being a soldier meets all three of these conditions. "Not only is it morally permissible for soldiers to kill enemy soldiers in combat," Kilner says, "but they are also morally obligated to use the force necessary to defend those who depend on them." He adds, "Because the moral responsibility for going to war lies with political authorities and because the political authorities' intentions are often opaque, soldiers should be largely immune from judgments about the just ends of war."[14]

However, while the military goes to great lengths to decode the psychology behind our natural aversion to killing, they balk at teaching troops about the moral justifications of combat killing, are not curious about understanding the connection between killing, guilt and PTSD and are not aggressive enough in treating these side effects once the mission is complete. A 2004 *New Yorker* article entitled "The Price of Valor," reflected on this willful ignorance: ". . . a number of observers inside and outside the Army worry that the high rate of close-up killing in Iraq has the potential to traumatize a new generation of veterans. Worse, they say, the Army and the Department of Veterans Affairs avoid thinking about it."[15] Or, as one Army public affairs officer said in 2002, "On the verge of war, we don't need to be talking about this upsetting thing."[16] To win wars, it is necessary to turn soldiers, at least for a time, "into reflexive, robotic killers." But, the problem is that the military will not take responsibility for the psychological effects that killing has on its combat troops. "I want that reflexive killing," an army captain wrote to Peter Kilner. "That serves me better in combat, but am I responsible for them after the fact?"

Dave Grossman believes that the military is responsible for what happens after the fact, saying that if "society prepares a soldier to overcome his resistance to killing and places him in an environment in which he will kill, then society has an obligation to deal forthrightly, intelligently, and morally with the psychological event."[17]

EXTENDED OR MULTIPLE DEPLOYMENTS

"People started having psychological problems. For pain, they gave you 800 milligrams of Motrin. But for psychological problems, they started handing out Prozac and Paxil. Their attitude was, suck it up. . . . People lose focus on the human component of being a soldier in harm's way. When you are told you are only going to be there for six months, and it keeps getting extended, and you watch the death toll go up, it does something to you."—National Guard Specialist Dave Bischel[18]

Another problem of the modern military that has become a particular concern in the wake of the Iraq War is that of multiple or extended deployments of combat troops. A February 2006 Le Moyne College/*Zogby International* poll found that three-quarters of troops in Iraq had served multiple tours.[19] Understandably, concern exists about the consequence of these multiple deployments on our all-volunteer force and their families. Vietnam veteran and retired Army Colonel Michael Doubler weighs the pros and cons: "You get a very experienced force, especially at the command level. And that is a very positive thing," he explains. "But it puts a lot of strain on the families. How much strain can they take? We don't know that, but we might be getting ready to find out."[20]

To deal with the stress of multiple deployments, the *San Diego Union-Tribune* reported in March 2006 that the Defense Department had been sending troops to war "with a cache of antidepressant and anti-anxiety medications." Senator Barbara Boxer had planned to address the practice the following month in her position on the Department of Defense Task Force on Mental Health, but the DOD missed the deadline to appoint panel members.[21] A month later, still waiting on the DOD, she wrote then Secretary of Defense Donald Rumsfeld, angrily saying, "I find it simply astonishing that the sheer magnitude of the mental health crisis facing our Armed Forces does not compel you to action."[22]

A second strike against the DOD in May 2006 came in the form of a GAO report which showed that only 22 percent of troops at risk for developing combat PTSD (as determined via the DOD's own post-deployment mental health screening form) had been referred for further mental health evaluations.[23] This was followed the same month by a stinging article in the *Hartford Courant* titled "Mentally Unfit, Forced To Fight." Conducting more than one hundred interviews with military family members and personnel, and reviewing reams of records obtained via Freedom of Information Act requests, the *Courant* uncovered numerous cases in which the military had failed to follow its own regulations in screening, treating and evacuating mentally unfit troops from Iraq. On top of this, severe psychological problems were disregarded in a number of instances as soldiers were kept in combat even after their superiors had become aware that they were showing signs of mental illness. The result of this was that one-in-five non-combat casualties in Iraq were suicides. The *Courant* investigation found that some of the service members who took their own lives between 2004 and 2005 "were kept on duty despite clear signs of mental distress, sometimes after being prescribed antidepressants with little or no mental health counseling or monitoring."[24]

In attempting to explain what was happening, Colonel Elspeth Ritchie, the Army's top medical expert, spoke about the practice of sending troops with PTSD back into the combat zone, admitting, "The challenge for us . . . is that the Army has a mission to fight. And, as you know, recruiting has been a challenge." She added, "And so we have to weigh the needs of the Army, the needs of the mission, with the soldiers' personal needs."[25]

Nancy Lessin, co-founder of Military Families Speak Out, remains unimpressed with the job the Pentagon is doing. "We have heard so much about what this military has learned in Vietnam [about PTSD], and how they're doing it differently now. And we don't see that at all." She adds, "We see the same mistakes happening—mistakes that are, in fact, not mistakes at all. It's really a way of denying this issue so they can keep as many warm bodies deployed and re-deployed."[26]

STRAINS

"There's a strange pressure on these soldiers not to have any problems with what they are doing. It's that old idea that a real man and a true warrior will stand strong."—Psychologist and trauma specialist Michael Phillips[27]

In addition to the problem with multiple or extended deployments, the nature of the modern battlefield places unique pressures, or strains, on the combat soldier. Prior to World War I, wars were more "reasonable," generally conducted during daylight hours in fixed positions between soldiers who were easily identified by the uniforms they wore. But things got unreasonable in a hurry as World War II ushered in nighttime warfare, Vietnam brought large-scale guerilla combat into being and our current wars introduced the modern asymmetric battlefield with its unbounded 360 degrees of vulnerability. This new type of warfare has in turn lead to three unique categories of combat strain: time, space and target.

Time strains result from continuous operations that leave soldiers with no opportunity to relax and unwind. Using night vision devices and other industrial age marvels, today's war machine conducts around the clock combat operations, rarely providing troops with the opportunity to get proper rest. As a result, fatigue and sleep deprivation are as much a part of the modern fighter's military experience as extended tours and stop-loss orders.*[28]

Extended or multiple deployments also exacerbate time strains. Psychiatrists Roy Swank and Walter Marchand, after combing through data on soldiers who had served in World War II, found that the mental condition of 98 percent of troops was adversely

---

* Stop-loss refers to troops who have fulfilled their commitment being forced to stay beyond it if deployed overseas; they may also have another 90 days tacked on to their commitment after returning home.

affected after only thirty-five days in combat.[29] Eric Massa, a 24-year naval officer and special assistant to NATO's former Supreme Allied Commander General Wesley Clark, summed it up by saying:

> Unlike most conflicts where only front line troops face hostile fire, nearly all our service members in Iraq are being exposed to constant fear . . . on a 24/7 basis for periods often lasting over a year at a time. The constant fear of dying is overwhelming and it is taking its toll. They say the average infantryman in WW2 saw 44 days of action; the rest of the time was training and transportation.[30]

Space strains develop in battlefield conditions that do not have traditional front or rear lines, and therefore do not allow troops adequate breaks from combat. Space strains are often exacerbated by the negative environmental factors that today's troops experience. Serving with the 5th Battalion, 3rd Field Artillery Regiment, Army Specialist Joseph Suell wrote a letter to his mother describing the hardship of living without electricity or having a chance to bathe for weeks on end. He also confessed worry about being killed by an enemy sniper. On June 16, 2003, the day after Father's Day, the husband and father of two overdosed on a bottle of painkillers. He was 24-years old.[31]

Target strains occur because of guerilla warfare conditions that make it difficult to distinguish enemy from civilian. In addition, orders to keep convoys moving forward—no matter what or who gets in the way—as well as mediation duties that require soldiers to listen to the frustrations of the civilian population while often not having the tools to help them, ups the pressure of target strains even more, often with fatal results. On August 10, 2006, a 19-year-old British private, Jason Chelsea, took an overdose of painkillers and slit his wrists after his superiors had advised him that he would be expected to shoot young suicide bombers once he got to Iraq. "I can't go out there and shoot at young children," he wrote in a letter to his mother, "I just can't go to Iraq. I don't care what side they are on. I can't do it."[32]

THE NEW FACE OF THE TROOPS

"If you tried to pull women out of the equation, this country could not fight a war."—Lory Manning, a retired Navy captain and director of the Women's Research and Education Institute[33]

Although they have appeared in every major war in U.S. history, the women serving in Afghanistan and Iraq constitute the largest female deployment ever to a combat zone, as one out of every seven soldiers is a woman. Since 2002, approximately 155,000 women have served, accounting for over 15 percent of the active duty force.[34] And while eight women died in the whole of the Vietnam War, through the beginning of 2007, 75 female warriors had paid the ultimate sacrifice while deployed to Afghanistan or Iraq, while over four hundred have been seriously injured. Despite President Bush's pledge of "no women in combat," and current federal law that is meant to keep them far from conflict, women warriors are fighting and dying on today's battlefields.[35] Indeed, the Army's 3rd Infantry Division has been collocating (i.e., placing side-by-side) women with combat support units since February 2005.[36]

Since women suffer PTSD at rates twice that of men, there was a logical concern that women would be disproportionately afflicted during combat.[37] Early data seemed to confirm the worry. In July 2005, *Newsweek* reported that, "Roughly 85,000 vets from the ongoing conflicts in Iraq and Afghanistan have sought VA medical care. Eleven percent—or 9,688—of those have been diagnosed with PTSD so far. Of those, 1,277 have been women. That adds up to a higher rate for women."[38]

Specialist Abbie Pickett arrived home from Iraq suffering from depression, sleeplessness, hyper-arousal and an inability to concentrate. At the age of seventeen, still in high school and believing that serving her country was a civic duty, Pickett had enlisted with the Wisconsin Army National Guard. Three months later, she attended her junior prom. By the age of twenty she was in Iraq, serving as a fuel truck driver for the 229th Combat Support Equipment Company, 4th Infantry Division. The assignment was risky, as convoys were the choice targets of roadside ambushes, and a 2,300-gallon fuel truck was a pretty big firecracker. "We went outside the wire everyday knowing that we may not come back," Pickett remembered.[39]

Based in Baquabah, near Tikrit, it would be not convoy duty, but an October 2003 shelling of her own base that would unmask the trauma of combat to Pickett. She was driving four of her badly injured fellow battle buddies to the base hospital when it came under attack. "All we could do was throw our bodies over the patients," Pickett recalled. Although she was physically unharmed, she felt shell-shocked by the experience.[40]

When she returned to Wisconsin in April 2004, her resulting PTSD cut short her plans to become a physician's assistant. Eventually, she dropped out of her college classes and began taking medication for sleeplessness. But she had trouble getting appointments with VA counselors due to the backlog of patients. Even getting to the VA was a pain. "The closest place I have to go for help is 90 miles away," Pickett said. "You have to make it easy for troops. Especially when it's hard enough just to get up in the morning." Pickett says she knows of many fellow soldiers who have committed suicide following their tours of duty.

Currently, she keeps busy doing outreach on college campuses while traveling with the advocacy group Iraq and Afghanistan Veterans of America. Of her stateside work, she says, "At first when you arrive at the campus and look out into the crowd, you see a sea of faces that aren't sure what to expect. They don't seem to be too interested in what we're going to say." But then something happens. "I tell my story and that's when I see their faces change. They start to ask their questions . . . many of which are quite good." You can see the pride and satisfaction in her face at making the war a bit more "real" to others. "I feel I've really been able to connect with them," Pickett beams.[41]

THE NEW FACE OF THE TROOPS, PART II

"For reservists, we're guys who have homes and jobs. We're hoping . . . we can be here for six months and be done with it."—Marine Reservist 1st Sgt. Dave Foster, days before the Iraq invasion began.[42]

Florida National Guardsman John Crawford was part of the initial invasion of Iraq in March of 2003. He returned home to pen a *New York Times* bestseller, *The Last True Story I'll Ever Tell*, which told of the frustrations unique to the reservist, or "weekend warrior" serving in the Middle East:

> We crossed the berm the same day as the army's Third Infantry Division, leading the invasion of Iraq. [But] when the Third Division was sent home, our National Guard unit was passed around the armed forces like a virus: the 108th Airborne, First Marine Expeditionary, 101st Airborne, and finally the Armored Division. They were all sent home, heroes of the war. Meanwhile, my unit stayed on, my soul rotting, our unit outlasted by no one in our tenure there.

> The Florida National Guard, forgotten, unnoticed—at one point the government even declared that we had been pulled out of Baghdad and brought home, although all around us the capital of our enemy seethed.[43]

National Guard and Reserve troops presently make up 40 percent of the frontline forces in Iraq and over 50 percent in Afghanistan. Some states have had 75 percent of their Guard activated; and they, along with the Reserve, are serving in combat roles on foreign shores at the highest rate in U.S. history.[44] Joining them are members of the Air Force and the Navy, who are serving in ground combat roles in increasing numbers. It seems as if everyone's in the Army now!

While the families of those who serve in the Air Force and Navy have access to a comparatively large number of support options, the families of National Guard and Reserve troops lack the same support network to help navigate the ravel of combat deployment. As a result, Guard and Reserve members are more at risk for PTSD, as 20 percent of Army National Guard troops in transport and non-medical support show symptoms of ASD or PTSD, while the figure for those serving in the Army Reserves rockets to 34 percent.[45]

In his research on Iraq War veterans, Charles Moskos, professor emeritus of sociology at Northwestern University and one of the premier sociological observers of the U.S. military, has discovered a number of stressors that are unique to Guard and Reserve troops, which may help shed light on the increased PTSD risk found in these groups. Among the triggers that Moskos discovered include:

- Frustration at serving longer in combat than active-duty troops, often without having an idea of when they'll be able to come home
- Disillusion at being used as "individual augmentees" or

fillers into units they haven't trained with, breaking the "unit cohesion" buffer to stress

- Worry over leaving loved ones behind with little support services
- Dissatisfaction with their inferior training and equipment compared to active forces, making them feel like second-class soldiers
- Aggravation with the stop-loss policy, which affects them more than it does active forces
- Anger that civilian contractors get paid three times more for doing the same job and have superior battle dress uniforms
- Financial penalty for long deployments, including fear over (or actuality of) losing their civilian job or small business while in combat[46]

In addition to the above concerns, a new Army policy was put in place in 2004 to target reserve officers who attempt to resign their commission. Stating that reserve officers are appointed "for an indefinite term and are held during the pleasure of the President," this policy has been used to circumvent the supposed eight-year limit on service in the reserves. As a consequence, over 400 reserve officers have had their resignations refused since 2004. Several officers have filed lawsuits in an attempt to win their discharge papers. "What the Army is saying is even though you are promised up front eight years as a reserve officer, they are saying they can keep you as long as they desire," said Stuart Slotnick, a lawyer representing one of the officers who is suing the Army.[47]

For those reserve officers who are allowed to return to their disrupted lives, reintegration is not always smooth. Lieutenant Brandon Ratliff, a six-time decorated executive officer of the Army Reserve's 909th Forward Surgical Team, had been employed by the

Department of Health in Columbus, Ohio, for nine years when he left for Afghanistan in September 2002. Before his departure, the DOH had offered him a promotion that he understood would be waiting for him when he returned home. But when he got back from Afghanistan in June 2003, he was told that he had not officially accepted the offer, and that the position had been filled. "He felt he was being punished because he had gone to war," explained his mother, Susan Coats. "He felt really ostracized. He wasn't asking for parties. He wasn't asking for recognition. He was just asking to pick up where he left off."[48]

While in Afghanistan, Ratliff had rescued injured soldiers on the frontline, but he couldn't save himself once back in America. Angry at the battles with the DOH, Ratliff shot and killed himself on March 18, 2004. Before pulling the trigger, he had sent an email to *The Columbus Dispatch*, saying, "I didn't think that I'd have to fight over there and come back and fight these guys, too."[49]

8. IDEALISM, GUILT AND THE DEGENERATION OF WAR

"Treat them with humanity, and let them have no reason to complain of our copying the brutal example of the British army in the treatment of our unfortunate brethren."—George Washington, ordering the humane treatment of hundreds of surrendering Hessian soldiers after the Battle of Trenton on Christmas Day, 1776.

HONOR AND DISILLUSIONMENT

A seasoned military veteran, Marine Sergeant Jeffrey Lehner served in both the first Gulf War and in Operation Enduring Freedom in Afghanistan. As part of the Marine Aerial Refueler Transport Squadron 352, Lehner and the "Raiders" played a key role hauling troops and cargo as the war began in the fall of 2001. On January 9, 2002, "Raider 04," a KC-130 refueling plane, crashed into a Pakistani mountain. All seven on board perished, making it, at the time, the deadliest single day for American forces. The crash also claimed the first female casualty in the post-9/11 era, Sergeant Jeannette L. Winters.[1]

The crash victims were all from Lehner's unit. In fact, he too would have died had he not been removed from the passenger manifest at the last moment. "The man who replaced him that night as flight engineer left behind a wife and three children," remembers Sarah Farmer, Lehner's fiancée at the time. "Jeff never forgave himself for not being on that plane." In addition to his guilt, he was haunted by the memory of having to retrieve the victims' body parts.[2]

Yet, the guilt Lehner felt over the crash was nothing compared to the psychological blowback he experienced after witnessing the interrogation techniques that his fellow soldiers were using in Afghanistan. In 2004, Lehner told a *Los Angeles Times* reporter that "detainees were being interrogated and tortured, and . . . were sometimes given psychotropic drugs." He also believed that some of the detainees had died in the custody of CIA special operations officers after they were put "in cargo containers aboard planes and interrogated ... while circling in the air." As a flight engineer, Lehner had flown on some of these flights and was distressed to discover that most of the detainees were not Taliban or al Qaeda. "By the time we got there, the serious fighters were long gone." The article's author, Ann Louise Bardach, didn't know what to make of Lehner's accounts. "[A]t the time, I hadn't heard of such abuses in Afghanistan," she said. "Such allegations were not yet being reported—and many Americans would probably have found his accusations unimaginable."[3]

After all that he had seen and experienced in Afgahnistan, Lehner knew that he needed help. When he returned home at the end of 2004, he admitted himself to a VA hospital for intensive PTSD treatment. But the PTSD ward was full, so he instead was placed with schizophrenic and bipolar patients. The following day, he asked Farmer to come get him. Eventually, he was put in touch with the "only psychologist trained in treating post-traumatic stress disorder for all returning veterans who live between L.A. and San Francisco," and signed up for outpatient/group therapy.[4]

Jim Nolan, a Vietnam veteran from Lehner's support group, said that Lehner was dealing with "anxiety, deeply frightening thoughts, and a sense of helplessness," mostly from guilt over not being able "to stop what he knew to be morally wrong." Dragged down by the burdens he had brought home with him from the Middle East, on December 7, 2005, Lehner shot his 77-year-old father and then turned the gun on himself, thus becoming another victim of the postwar psychological struggle that occurs when soldiers are forced to witness or commit immoral acts on the battlefield. While the actual requirements of fighting are difficult enough for most soldiers to cope with, the additional struggle of dealing with the morality of what they have seen or done can lead to terrible consequences, as was the case with Lehner. Unfortunately, the changes in American policy toward treatment of prisoners of war that has occurred under the Bush administration is only making things worse.

THE SLIPPERY SLOPE

"All my life, we were the good guys. We were the standard-bearers for human rights. We were the ones telling the Russians not to treat people like we now treat people. We decried what went on in Chile. We decried the disappearances in Argentina. Now we're disappearing people. It scares me. The terrorists didn't take anything from us—except several thousand lives, and I don't diminish that. But all of our loss of human rights we have done to ourselves."—Jeff Davis, Vietnam veteran and registered Republican[5]

In September 2006, Congress returned from its summer recess to briefly debate and quickly pass the Military Commissions Act. The bill gave the president sole authority to interpret the Geneva Conventions, and also dissolved Habeas Corpus protections for "terrorists and other unlawful enemy combatants."[6] Crafted as an end run around the Hamdan vs. Rumsfeld Supreme Court ruling that had decreed the military commissions set up to try Guantánamo detainees as "violat [ing] both the Uniform Code of Military Justice and the four Geneva Conventions," the new bill sought to legitimize new American "tools" for fighting terrorism, among them: "secret detention, enforced disappearance, prolonged incommunicado detention, indefinite detention without charge, arbitrary detention, and torture or other cruel, inhuman or degrading treatment."[7]

Former Secretary of State Colin Powell, the only Bush Cabinet official to have seen combat, described the grave risks of this new direction in American policy: "If you just look at how we are perceived in the world and the kind of criticism we have taken over Guantánamo, Abu Ghraib and renditions," he said in the days before the Senate vote, "whether we believe it or not, people are now starting to question whether we're following our own high standards."[8] In the book *On Killing*, author Dave Grossman talks about how, historically, America has always been looked at as a country that upheld high moral values in warfare:

> One interviewer of World War II POWs told me that German soldiers repeatedly told him that relatives with World War I combat experience had advised, 'Be brave, join the infantry, and surrender to the first Americans you see.' The American reputation for fair play and respect for human life had survived over generations, and the decent actions of American soldiers in World War I had saved the lives of many soldiers in World War II.[9]

However, if those at the top now refuse to obey long-established laws and rules, what can we expect from those who serve below them? More ominously, how will our new playbook affect the short and long-term psychological welfare of our service members? If we use the case of Jeffrey Lehner as a guide, there is going to be a lot of trouble in the months and years to come.

DÉNOUEMENT OF A NEBULOUS WAR

> *"[Some of] the morale issues that have come to public attention in OIF have revolved around reserve units. The most notable has been the prison abuse scandal of the 327nd Military Police Company (based in Maryland) in Abu Ghraib. There was also the [October 2004] case of the reservists in the 343rd Quartermaster Company (based in South Carolina) who refused orders to deliver fuel on the grounds their vehicles were inadequately armored and the fuel to be delivered was contaminated."*—Charles Moskos, professor emeritus of sociology at Northwestern University[10]

On June 4, 2005, a 44-year-old Army colonel committed suicide in a military base trailer near the airport in Baghdad. Ted S. Westhusing, who shot himself once in the head with his service pistol, was at that time the highest-ranking officer to die in Iraq. A leading scholar of military ethics and a professor at West Point, Westhusing had volunteered for war duty in part to keep what he taught real and legitimate. While training police in Iraq, however, the colonel had uncovered corruption by U.S. contractors. "In e-mails to his family, [he] seemed especially upset by one conclusion he had reached: that traditional military values such as duty, honor, and country had been replaced by profit motives in Iraq," the *Los Angelese Times* reported. In a letter found in his trailer after his suicide, one question loomed large for him: "How is honor possible in a war like the one in Iraq?"[11]

More than a year later, in August 2006, bristling as the debate grew in America over the justification and handling of the war, former Secretary of Defense Donald Rumsfeld delivered what *Washington Post* opinion columnist William M. Arkin christened a "fire-and-brimstone speech," declaring that "any moral or intellectual confusion about who and what is right or wrong can weaken the ability of free societies to persevere."[12] Ten days before Rumsfeld's speech, *Time* magazine had published an article called "Putting the Iraq War on Trial" about Army Lieutenant Ehren Watada, the first commissioned officer to refuse orders to deploy to Iraq. Watada, a member of the 3rd Brigade, 2nd Infantry Division based out of Fort Lewis, had signed up for military service in the wake of September 11, 2001. He served at first with distinction in South Korea and, while initially supportive of the invasion of Iraq, he eventually came to believe that the war was unlawful. As a result, he felt that he had a duty as an officer to disobey what he considered an illegal order. At first, he tried to resign his commission, but the Army wouldn't let him. He then asked to be sent instead to Afghanistan, a war he supported, but his request was denied.[13] "I feel that we have been lied to and betrayed by this administration," Watada told a *Seattle Times* reporter in June 2006, adding:

> [The] war in Iraq violates our democratic system of checks and balances. It usurps international treaties and conventions that by virtue of the Constitution become American law. The wholesale slaughter and mistreatment of the Iraqi people with only limited accountability is not only a terrible moral injustice, but a contradiction to the Army's own Law of Land Warfare. My participation would make me party to war crimes.[14]

During his Article 32 hearing (which is the investigation before a case is referred to a general court martial), in August 2006, the Army prosecutor, among other accusations, said that Watada had shown contempt for President Bush by saying that the President had "lied to service members" and the nation to justify the invasion of Iraq. Eric Seitz, one of Watada's lawyers, fired back by saying that Watada's stance against the war had been courageous. "It's not our intention to put the war on trial, but the nature of the trial makes it necessary."[15] Watada's first court martial, in February 2007, ended in a mistrial, but the Army announced that a second court martial would begin in July. [16]

The case of Ehren Watada vividly illustrates what happens when our government abdicates its responsibility to fight wars that are just and necessary (and then fights them only as a last resort) and instead wages war based on dubious or questionable premises. What are the emotional effects on the men and women who are sent to fight in such wars? How do they deal with the issues of necessity, legality and morality? How do they rectify the idealism of serving their country when they feel that their government is lying to them? And how do they deal with the strains of fighting in such a war when they return home?

VIOLENCE AND ATROCITY

> "[T]he Vietnam War, with its 'permanent free-fire zones,'
> technological overkill, and daily 'body count,' was the very sort of
> matrix of 'disorder and absurdity' from which evil is born: 'My Lai
> illuminates, as nothing else has, the essential nature of America's
> war in Vietnam ... In the starkness of its murders and the
> extreme dehumanization experienced by victimizers and imposed
> on victims, My Lai reveals to us how far America has gone along
> the path of deadly illusion."—Dr. Robert Jay Lifton[17]

As author Edward Tick explains, "When women and children are willing to die to stop us, and we cannot distinguish between enemies and civilians because an entire population resists us, then our soldiers' belief in our goodness cracks—and so does their spirit."[18] In April 2006, the spirit of Ryan Briones certainly cracked. Less than thirty six hours after returning from his second tour of Iraq, Briones was charged with stealing a pickup truck, crashing it into a house, leaving the scene of the accident, driving under the influence and resisting arrest. Awarded a Purple Heart for injuries received in Fallujah on his first deployment, it was the strain of what he had seen on his second tour that cast the longer shadow, as it was on that tour that Briones was involved in what is known as the Haditha atrocity.

The Haditha atrocity began with the death of Lance Corporal Miguel "TJ" Terrazas—Briones' best friend—on November 19, 2005. Responding to the explosion of a roadside bomb outside of Kilo Company's Firm Base Sparta, Briones and his team arrived at the scene to find the remains of Terrazas, still sitting in the destroyed Humvee in which he had been riding, his body split in half. "He had a giant hole in his chin. His eyes were rolled back up in his skull," Briones later recalled.[19]

The Marines immediately began a sweep of nearby homes, looking for information about the identity of the bomber. At some point during the sweep, the Marines entered three different homes and killed all the people inside. Iraqi citizens who witnessed the killings later said that the Marines shot "men, women and children at close range." According to Rep. John Murtha, the "Marines overreacted . . . and killed innocent civilians in cold blood."[20]

Briones didn't witness any of this, however, as he was busy, along with another member of his team, rescuing two other Marines who had been pinned down under their vehicle after the explosion. After transporting the wounded men to a nearby soccer field, where a Black Hawk helicopter scooped them out of danger, Briones and his team went back to the base, where, as Briones later recalled, "[a] lot of people were mad. Everyone had just had a [terrible] feeling about what had happened to T.J."[21]

Later that day, Briones' team was called back to the explosion site and ordered to mark the bodies of the civilian casualties before body bagging them. After doing that, Briones and another Marine, Lance Corporal Andrew Wright, were ordered to photograph the corpses with their personal cameras. Moving the body of one young girl, Briones watched in horror as the insides of her brain poured onto his legs.

The photos later became the focus of questions by investigators who interviewed Briones in March, shortly before he returned home. "They wanted to know if the bodies had been moved or tampered with," Briones recalled. Eventually, after pressure from *Time* magazine, which had conducted its own investigation into the killings, in December 2006, four Marines were charged "with murder in the killings of two dozen Iraqi civilians, including at least 10 women and children, in the village of Haditha." In addition, four officers, including a lieutenant colonel in charge of the 1st Marine Regiment's 3rd Battalion, were charged with "dereliction of duty and failure to ensure that accurate information about the killings was delivered up the Marine Corps' chain of command."[22]

What had made those Marines snap? Jonathan Shay, in *Achilles in Vietnam: Combat Trauma and the Undoing of Character* offers that, among the events "that drive soldiers berserk are . . . death of a friend-in-arms . . . [and] seeing dead comrades who have been mutilated by the enemy."[23] The Marines at Haditha certainly experienced those triggers. In addition, most of them were on their third tours of duty, and had previously taken part in Fallujah's Operation Phantom Fury, one of the most vicious battles of the entire war. Did the level of violence they had seen and unleashed on their previous tours have anything to do with their behavior in Haditha? Did repeated deployments to Iraq cause the Marines to buckle? Or did the breakdown at Haditha stem from the unique pressures and features of the Iraq War itself? Writer Thomas Ricks says that while our military "was the finest fighting force in the world for conventional combat . . . it was ill-prepared for the irregular war in which it found itself [in Iraq and Afghanistan]. In this sense, abusive soldiers sometimes were victims of the Army's lack of preparation."[24]

Whatever the specific reasons for the Marines going over the edge in Haditha, the real cause of tragedies like this is the innumerable and senseless mistakes that have been made along the command chain in Iraq and Afghanistan, which brutally mirror similar mistakes that were made in Vietnam. Robert Jay Lifton expounded on this idea in his discussions of Vietnam, and his observations still resonate today:

> Most of the harmful behavior that occurs in Vietnam is due to the malignant environment we create there, an environment of murder. For instance the men who killed at My Lai, let's say, had no discernible or diagnosable psychiatric disease. They were, I would say, in an advanced state of brutalization and under enormous pressures. The kind of thing that could happen to any one of us, were we put under similar training and that kind of situation.[25]

Author Chris Hedges expounds on the psychological twisting of once idealistic warriors, saying, "To be sure, soldiers who kill innocents pay a tremendous personal emotional and spiritual price. But within the universe of total war, equipped with weapons that can kill hundreds or thousands of people in seconds, soldiers only have time to reflect later. By then these soldiers often have been discarded, left as broken men in a civilian society that does not understand them and does not want to understand them."[26] The incompetence and negligence of those in charge forces us to ask the question, just as we did forty years ago in Vietnam, "Did our troops fail us or did we fail them?"

After returning home, Briones and Wright tried to keep the dark spirits of that Haditha night at bay, but the events "remain[ed] seared in their memories."[27] Both men were repeatedly interviewed regarding what had happened, each military review refreshing the effects of the trauma, with little follow-up support offered. "That's what hurts," said Briones' mother, Susie. "They want these kids to serve their country, but they won't back them up."[28]

STARING DOWN THE BARREL

He wasn't an important person, but he was very important to us. What's important is what happened to him when he came back.—Joyce Lucey, mother of Jeffrey Lucey[29]

On March 18, 2003, Lance Corporal Jeffrey Lucey celebrated his 22nd birthday at Camp Shuiba in Kuwait. That same morning, President Bush had ordered Saddam Hussein to leave Iraq or face attack, saying, "All the decades of deceit and cruelty have now reached an end."[30]

Coming from a family where military service and sacrifice was common, Lucey had set out to become a Marine to prove himself. "He claimed it was for the benefits," his father said, "but it was more a proving something to himself, that he could go through the toughest [trials] and succeed."[31] While the physical tests were intense, the mental challenges, Lucey later came to find out, were stumbling blocks of an entirely different order.

On March 20, 2003, Lucey jotted down the following note in a small camouflage-covered notebook:

At 10:30 p.m. a scud landed in our vicinity. We were just falling asleep when a shock wave rattled through our tent. The noise was just short of blowing out your eardrums.

Everyone's heart truly skipped a beat and the reality of where we are and what's truly happening hit home.[32]

The following day, America rolled into Iraq. Part of the 6th Motor Transport Battalion, 4th Force Service Support Group, Lucey was part of a crew responsible for keeping the 80,000-member battalion fueled and fed.[33] At the controls of his heavy convoy truck, Lucey transported ammunition, food, water and occasionally, Iraqi prisoners of war. It was dangerous work, with the convoys frequently being fired upon. Lance Corporal Mike Wetherbee, who served in Iraq with Lucey, described what it was like transporting prisoners:

> Moving POWs was, at times, disturbing. MPs would load them on trucks, hands bound behind their backs, sometimes with bags over their heads, often without any food or water. The drivers . . . would occasionally share their provisions with the 15 or so prisoners confined to each truck. The few who could speak English would tell their Marine drivers about being forced to join the Iraqi army; if they refused, family members would be shot, one at a time, until they changed their minds.[34]

In addition to the pressures of doing his job, Lucey's distress was increased by orders that he was to run over anything that got in the way of his convoy. "Hit 'em. Crush 'em," drivers were told, as if they were simply "bumps in the road." The resulting stress from all of this caused Lucey's disillusionment to build. On April 18, 2003, he wrote to his girlfriend, "I have done so much immoral shit during the last month that life is never going to seem the same, and all I want is to erase the past month, pretend it didn't happen."

When Lucey's five months in Iraq ended, he returned to Camp Pendleton with the rest of the 4th FSSG. His journals exposed the torment of what he had experienced, as he described seeing "dead people, not dead soldiers." When he tried to share his anguish, a fellow Marine told him, "If you keep talking like that, you'll not be able to go back home. You'll have to stay here [at Camp Pendleton] from two to four months." Lucey was anxious to get back home, so he kept his mouth shut.

Although there is confusion over some of the statements made by Lucey (the military investigated and determined that he could neither have seen nor done some of the things he claimed), upon his return home, what he had experienced in Iraq began to slowly chip away at his soul. He spoke of lifting a dead boy's body from the side of the road and being ordered to kill two POWs in cold blood. His parents have committed to sharing their son's story in order to help other families better understand the warning signs of PTSD. Their recollections evidence Lucey's pain:

> Jeff would talk of his frequent/intrusive memories of combat with a distant gaze and a monotone, flat voice trailing off as he would recount his experiences. He had memories/dreams of being in alleyways, being chased, killing, etc. He shouted out in his sleep.

> Jeff followed the war issue closely after returning . . . He talked of the public seeing only what a certain few wanted them to see, of how they had to bury bodies, body parts and even sweep and turn over the bloodied sand before the press arrived.

> He never became angry with family, but he would at the war, the Bush administration and the VA. He felt different—as if he did not belong here. He also felt as if going crazy. He was feeling things which made no sense and he knew it and could not resolve this conflict.

As time went on, a sense of isolation began to appear to the point that he was becoming reclusive—his world was shrinking to that of the kitchen and the bedroom. The feelings of disconnect worsened horribly. His relationship with his girlfriend fell apart.

Jeff stated that he had to drink so much so that he could pass out and sleep. Marijuana use was to take the edge off and calm. He was also on prescribed medication.

On Christmas Eve, 2003, Jeff informed his sister while he was drunk that he was nothing more than a murderer. He spoke of the incident of killing two men. When he spoke of this incident, it was as if he was traveling back across time to that exact moment, his rifle shaking, the fear, terror [he was seeing] in their eyes/faces, the splattering of bone and blood.

After eight months, suicidal thoughts (at least to our knowledge) became the only means of escaping the pain, guilt, terrors. Then when the chaos of PTSD became overwhelming and made him feel even more like a failure, he felt as if this was his only option.[35]

The Lucey's tried desperately to get their son the help that he needed. Because he was concerned that the VA would tell the Marines that he was having problems, and was worried about ruining his job prospects if his PTSD was publicly revealed, he saw a private therapist. He continued, however, to slide further into depression.

Eventually, his paranoia and hyper-vigilance made him so jumpy and embarrassed that he dropped out of college. He also heard voices and felt hands touching him, and kept a flashlight nearby at night to keep the imagined camel spiders at bay. One night, he sneaked out of the house, and in full camouflage uniform went down to a store, armed with a pellet gun. Kevin and Joyce Lucey wonder now if he was attempting to commit "suicide by cop," where a person tries to force the police to kill him.

Finally, against his will, his parents brought him in to the local VA Hospital. Four days later, he was released. "They told him to stay sober and then they would assess him for PTSD," his parents recall.[36] Two days after getting home from the hospital, he crashed his a car between two trees. "He was sliding fast. It was one event after another," said Joyce Lucey. "You didn't get a chance to catch your breath . . ." His pain was so great that at twenty-three years of age, the Marine who had seen combat in Iraq asked his father one day if he could sit in his lap. For almost an hour, Jeff sat silently curled up as though he were a young boy. "The therapist said he was regressing," said his mother, "looking for a safe place."[37]

Eventually, he started dropping hints about committing suicide. He told his sister he had already chosen a rope and a tree, but then quickly assured her, "I would never do it because it would hurt mom and dad."[38] On day, he frightened his mother by asking her to listen to a song called "45" by Shinedown:

What ever happened to the young man's heart
Swallowed by pain, as he slowly fell apart
Swimming through the ashes of another life
No real reason to accept the way things have changed
Staring down the barrel of a 45

On June 22, 2004, Kevin Lucey returned home from work and knew instantly that something was wrong. He found his son hanging in the basement. The guilt and pain in the young man's heart had ended.

PART III— A CALL TO ARMS

"The physical war is over. The mental war has just begun."—Private First Class Herold Noel, homeless Iraq veteran, in the documentary *When I Come Home*[1]

9. RETURNING TO A FOREIGN WORLD

"Since the Revolutionary War, Americans have promised to take care of their wounded soldiers. If we decide we can't afford to do that, if we decide that the cost has simply become too high, and I would suggest that it has always been too high, then what we are saying is that we can no longer afford to use soldiers to solve our problems."—Penny Coleman, author of *Flashback: Posttraumatic Stress Disorder, Suicide, and the Lessons of War*[1]

A PLEA FOR UNDERSTANDING

Specialist Douglas Barber, an Army reservist with the 1485th Transportation Company of the Ohio National Guard, deployed to Iraq in the summer of 2003, where he served for seven months, spending most of his time driving a truck between the Baghdad Airport and a Balad military base. Like many reservists who are sent to the front lines, Barber was not properly prepared for what he had to face. "It was really bad—death was all around you, all the time. You couldn't escape it," he said in an interview.[2]

Upon his return home, things began to fall apart. His personality changed, ("[h]e was a really good guy, pretty level-headed . . . when he came back from Iraq the difference in him was so sad," a friend recalled) and he split from his wife of eleven years. Eventually, he was diagnosed with PTSD and put on Clonazepam, an anti-anxiety drug that can cause depression. However, things continued to deteriorate for him. In early January 2006 he wrote an entreaty to the American people, saying that,

> I myself have trouble coping with an everyday routine that deals with other people that often causes me to have a short fuse. A lot of soldiers lose multiple jobs just because they are trained to be killers and they have lived in an environment that is conducive to that. We are always on guard for our safety and that of our comrades. When you go to bed at night you wonder, will you be sent home in a flag draped coffin because a mortar round went off on your sleeping area?[3]

A few days later, on January 16, 2006, Barber changed his answering machine message ("If you're looking for Doug, I'm checking out of this world. I'll see you on the other side"), phoned the police, then went out onto the porch with his shotgun. When the police would not release him from his pain by shooting him, he shot himself in the head.[4]

SPEED DEMONS

> *"War stories end when the battle is over or when the soldier comes home. In real life, there are no moments amid smoldering hilltops for tranquil introspection. When the war is over, you pick up your gear, walk down the hill and back into the world."*
> —John Crawford, Iraq veteran[5]

The feelings that Douglas Barber described—"coping with an everyday routine ... a short fuse ... on guard ..." graphically illustrate one of the major problems that many veterans have in re-entering the regular world after serving in combat: that of replacing the adrenalinized "war rush." In battle, things move at a rapid fire pace, as speed can mean the difference between life and death. Black Hawk medevac pilots whisking wounded troops to the hospital have saved countless lives, as has timely forward medical care. One of the few bright spots in the Iraq war is the wounded-to-killed ratio, which stands at about 8-to-1, vs. 3-to-1 in Vietnam, which can be attributed to the speed at which care is provided to wounded soldiers. However, while speed can save lives, it can crush them too, particularly when troops are forced to slow down upon their return to civilian life.[6] "The quickening tempos of military life are indeed one of the most worrisome factors for our military leadership," says retired Major H.C. Peterson Jr.[7]

The increased speed of warfare also goes hand-in-hand with the adrenaline surge that soldiers experience in combat. "There's some evidence that it has something to do with addiction to the adrenaline rush, which may have a physical as well as an emotional component," says PTSD specialist Dr. Arthur Blank.[8] Many veterans miss that rush upon their return to civilian life. "The biggest adjustment is going from 18-hour days, seven days a week, with no days off, to working a 40-hour week based on the clock," Iraq veteran Chris Baer says. "From that tempo to civilian life, it's incredibly slo-o-o-o-w."[9] Jason Harvey, a soldier from the Fort Carson-based 2nd Brigade Combat Team, says, "When you're in combat, the adrenaline rush, it becomes fluid, you're used to it all the time. Then when you come back, it's not there anymore and you have to find something to get back to how it was." To replace that rush, many soldiers resort to doing extreme things that mimic the thrill and danger they experienced in warfare, like skydiving or rock climbing. Harvey, who was kicked out of the army after being found with a loaded gun and was later diagnosed with PTSD, drove his car at high speeds and played paint ball to duplicate the feelings he had had in combat. "It might sound strange, but for me, when I was driving fast, it made me calm again," he recalled.[10]

While activities like paint ball are harmless, many veterans will go to great lengths in trying to duplicate the wartime rush, often with tragic results. In the two years following the first Persian Gulf War, for example, it was discovered that returning vets had a 9.4 percent higher death rate than other service members, with most of the deaths being caused by accidents such as car wrecks. In 2006, over 150 sailors and Marines died in off-duty accidents. "This has been one of the worst years in recent history," said Commander Edward Hobbs, a spokesman for the Centers for Disease Control and Prevention. Other branches of the military have reported similar results. Unfortunately, veterans cannot simply flick a switch and turn off the rush that they are used to experiencing in battle once they return home. "They can't just turn their adrenaline off after 365 days of surviving," says Steve Robinson of Veterans for America.[11] And this is not an historical anomaly, as veterans who served in the Vietnam War had a 7 percent higher death rate after discharge than veterans who did not serve.

Another speed-related feature of combat that soldiers often bring home with them is what is known as hyper-vigilance. In the combat environment, even the smallest, seemingly most insignificant thing can turn deadly. As a result, soldiers must be hyperaware of their environment at all times. When they return home, even though they are no longer in harm's way, many veterans remain at a high level of vigilance, which leads them to do things like constantly check rooms or streets for signs of danger, even though none exist. Hyper-vigilance (along with re-experiencing and avoidance) is one of the three major signs in determining if someone suffers from PTSD.[12]

A final area where speed negatively affects our returning combat troops is the quickness at which they are able to get from the battlefront to the home front. Up through the Korean War, the slowness of travel ensured a gradual re-entry for the soldier returning from combat. Plodding along by horse or train or ship meant that, instead of being thrown back into society without a chance to decompress and process their wartime experiences, soldiers could spend time dealing with what they had experienced in a safe and quarantined environment.

But the development of air travel has short-circuited this important element of the healing process. Beginning with the Vietnam War, the time for built-in purification rituals began to fall away. Instead of taking the slow boat home, the veteran "was flown back quickly by himself, moving from the blood and gore of the combat zone to his hometown in the space of twenty-four hours."[13] This has had a negative effect on the combat soldier, as they no longer have the necessary time to transition from life on the battlefield to life at home. "I had been in Baghdad one month and Brooklyn the next, and the adjustment was tough," recalled Paul Rieckhoff. "As I walked in New York City, stimuli overwhelmed me. People shouting, horns blowing, sirens wailing. It all seemed to reverberate inside my head like a Ping-Pong ball."[14]

According to author Ben Shephard, historically, troops that have come quickly have had more problems then those that were given time to re-acclimate. "It turned out that the people who had been reunited immediately with their families, their prognosis turned out to be worse than those people who'd had the time to be in, as it were, this decompression chamber before they were returned to the civilian world."[15]

CLEANSING RITUALS

"The first shamans earned their keep in primitive societies by providing explanations and rituals that enabled man to deal with his environment and his personal anguish. Early man, no less than we, dealt with forces that he could not understand or control, and he attempted to come to grips with his vulnerability by trying to bring order to his universe."
—Richard A. Gabriel in *No More Heroes*

Throughout history, societies have made "special efforts to protect or restore the souls of their warriors during times of war."[16] In the past, the need for acceptance, cleansing and forgiveness was recognized as important to the eventual well-being of the warrior. Richard A. Gabriel writes that:

[P]rimitive societies often required soldiers to perform purification rites before allowing them to rejoin their communities . . . Psychologically, these rituals provided soldiers with a way of ridding themselves of stress and the terrible guilt that always accompanies the sane after war. It was also a way of treating guilt by providing a mechanism through which fighting men could decompress and relive their terror without feeling weak or exposed. Finally, it was a way of telling the soldier that what he did was right and that the community for which he fought was grateful and that, above all, this community of sane and normal men welcomed him back.[17]

As an example of these cleansing rituals, Zulu fighters, after defeating the forces of the British Empire in an 1879 battle, "underwent many days of cleansing before they were free enough of their contagious pollution to be permitted to present themselves to King

Cetshwayo at the royal kraal."[18] As Edward Tick writes in *War and the Soul*, "tribal people realized that an entire society is afflicted by war and must participate in its warriors' healing."[19]

However, in contemporary western society, these healing and cleansing rituals have largely disappeared. "Most cultures provide rituals for the returning warrior," writes Peter J. Murphy, an Australian military psychologist. "[H]owever, modern Western society has tended to neglect these rituals and the meaning that accompanies them." While the traditional "Welcome Home" parade is a modern form of the cleansing ritual, and does show societal support for the returning warrior, it is a passive experience rather than something the veteran actively partakes in. As a consequence, its effects are temporary and fleeting. The cheering crowd returns home feeling that they have done their duty, and the vet is left to deal with the rest of the journey on his or her own.

But if the veteran has already been prepared, either through planned or unplanned decompression, their re-entry to civilian life is less jarring and more manageable. That is why, as a society, it is important for us to engage in cleansing rituals, as they provide a way for us to show approval for the wartime deeds of our soldiers. "Without such recognition and support," Murphy adds, "veterans may question their actions and face issues of guilt and lack of meaning."[20]

Unfortunately, in modern times, our social practices have broken down during the crucial reintegration period, which allows PTSD to fester in the dark corners of our warriors' minds. One of the most costly lessons of the post-Vietnam era was the denial of absolution and societal acceptance for returning veterans. A 1997 study found that "social variables," such as an anemic, and at times hostile, reception when they returned home, may have contributed to the eventual development of PTSD in many soldiers. "Veterans typically returned home after the most powerful emotional experience of their lives to find little acknowledgement and much misunderstanding by their families and society at large."[21]

While much of the reaction toward returning Vietnam veterans was the result of the war's unpopularity and ambiguous outcome, it is important to separate the war from the warrior, and realize that our negative feelings toward the former should never dilute our compassion toward the latter. As a nation, we cannot let our rising anger about the war spill over into our treatment of the troops.

STRUGGLING TO FIND A HOME

Another serious problem for veterans is that of homelessness, especially among those who are suffering from post-traumatic stress disorder. According to John Driscoll, communications director of the National Coalition for Homeless Veterans, "the key to a successful transition out of military life is a large support network of family, friends and service providers." Without that support network, veterans have problems orienting to civilian life.[22]

After the Vietnam War, thousands of veterans returned home to a hostile society that offered almost no appreciation for their wartime accomplishments, or more importantly, any services to deal with their PTSD. Consequently, to this day, thousands of Vietnam veterans still struggle with homelessness and substance abuse.[23] According to the Department of Veterans Affairs, about one-third of the adult homeless population is made up of veterans, and as many as 200,000 veterans are currently living on the streets or in shelters. Perhaps twice as many experience homelessness at some point during the course of a year, while many others are considered at risk because of poverty, lack of support from family and friends, and substandard living conditions. While some experts have questioned the degree to which PTSD causes homelessness, more than 70 percent of homeless veterans have some sort of mental or substance abuse problem that stems from PTSD.[24]

In many ways, today's returning veterans are coming home to a very different America than the one that Vietnam veterans encountered almost forty years ago. In addition to nearly unanimous support for their wartime service, there are approximately 250 nonprofit service organizations that provide housing, employment and counseling services to veterans.[25] However, in spite of this increased support system, these private organizations are not equipped financially or personnel wise to handle the expected onslaught of veterans that will be returning home in the coming years. And, the government isn't offering enough assistance to cover the gap. This is on top of the fact that both the VA and private veteran service organizations are already stretched thin providing services for veterans of previous conflicts.[26] According to the National Coalition for Homeless Veterans, an estimated 500,000 veterans were homeless during 2004, but the VA had the resources to tend to only 100,000 of them. Veteran organizations struggle to provide assistance to as many of the other 80 percent as possible, but the need far exceeds the available resources.[27]

Another major issue that today's veterans face is that housing costs have dramatically increased at the same time that wages have remained stable, which often makes rental housing unaffordable, especially in larger, more expensive cities. In addition, many soldiers are serving multiple tours with uncertain end dates, making it harder to hold onto a home or apartment.[28]

Furthermore, for many veterans, there is a gap of months, sometimes years, between when their military benefits end and their veterans' benefits begin.[29] Almost half of America's 2.7 million disabled veterans receive $337 or less a month in benefits, and fewer than one-tenth of them are rated 100 percent disabled, which provides them with $2,393 a month, tax free. The VA benefit system is also composed of confusing, bureaucratic layers that are difficult to navigate. For example, if a veteran is diagnosed as 70 percent disabled as a result of a physical ailment, and 30 percent disabled as a result of post-traumatic stress disorder, their total disability does not necessarily total 100 percent; it could amount to 80 percent. That would result in a monthly check of $1,277—a tiny amount in cities like New York, where studio apartments routinely exceed $1,000 a month.[30]

An online survey of 600 veterans by the non-profit group Amvets found that eight in ten felt that more could be done to help troops after they leave the military and join the workforce. Nearly four in ten felt underemployed, and two-thirds had trouble obtaining disability benefits.[31] Linda Boone, executive director of the National Coalition for Homeless Veterans, accurately sizes up the situation, saying: "People just assume that the VA takes care of all vets, but they don't. We don't spend enough money on homeless people in general, let alone veterans."[32]

To try to close the funding gap, in November 2006, the VA announced nearly $11.6 million in grants to public, private non-profit and faith-based groups for programs assisting homeless veterans.[33] However, this amount will barely make a dent in the projected $1 billion shortfall in health care funding that veterans' groups forecast for 2007.

OPEN WOUNDS

> "I have PTSD. It never leaves you. One might adjust. One might adapt and partially overcome, but it never leaves you. Each night. Each loud sound. Each time a helicopter passes over head. Each dream possesses the potential to take you back. To terrorize. To plunge the body into another [adrenaline] soaked rush. Oh, yeah, it sucks."—Former Vietnam veteran[34]

One of the most insidious consequences of the current wars in Iraq and Afghanistan is the effect it has on the psychological condition of veterans who fought in previous wars. The VA reports that PTSD disability claims have doubled since 2000 (with the lion's share added since 2003), and that 73 percent of these new cases are Vietnam veterans. To cite one high profile example, in August 2006, former senator and Vietnam veteran Max Cleland admitted seeking help for post-traumatic stress disorder that had been triggered by the war in Iraq.[35]

If there is one slim silver lining, however, it is that the struggles of Vietnam veterans are informing the way we deal with our current veterans. By sharing their hard-wrought experience, Vietnam veterans are helping to validate and confirm the feelings felt by today's returning troops. James Starowicz, a Vietnam veteran and member of Veterans for Peace, looks both backwards and forward as he talks about dealing with his newest brothers and sisters:

> We talked about fighting in those sands of those deserts, instead of the jungles and rivers that I faced while I was over in 'Nam. My memories came to the surface in the buildup to Gulf War I. More recently, watching the so-called Shock and Awe bombings brought back the demons of 'Nam, Korea and even World War II to vets of those wars. The invasion brought out the mind's pictures of past times, especially long pushed-back frames of memories thought already buried or completely forgotten.
>
> All who experience and live through any conflict have a complete change of mindset. Society as a whole quickly puts things such as that out of sight, out of mind. Society doesn't want to pay to repair what it's created—if it can even be done. We have lost valuable time, not to mention lives, because of the denial and our being an apathetic society to issues such as this.

These returning troops, once considered our little brothers and sister veterans, their military experiences having aged them well beyond their own generations, must be taken care of no matter the cost, and those Iraqi/Afghan citizens should also not be forgotten. It's our responsibility to cover all the damage created and to look long and hard before we engage once again in the carnage.[36]

The key to healing is to take hold of war's realities and use its lessons to give meaning to the trauma it creates. Political action and public engagement appeals to so many Vietnam (and now Afghanistan and Iraq) veterans because it helps them come to terms with their wartime experiences. With their activism, they dip back into the current of life, serving as witnesses to the painful tide of war, while attempting to find personal salvation and release.

FROM DARKNESS TO LIGHT

Captain Stefanie Pelkey was the first woman to serve in the 94th Field Artillery Battalion in Idar-Oberstein, Germany. On November 5, 2004 her husband, Captain Michael Jon Pelkey, who had served a yearlong tour with the 1st Armored Division in Iraq, committed suicide after struggling with PTSD-related symptoms. "My Michael was such a brave and dear heart. I wish he were here telling of his daily struggle with PTSD instead of me," Stefanie wrote in an email.[37]

Drawing on the internal strength that propelled her to be the first woman in an all-male combat unit, Pelkey has devoted her time and energy to creating something positive out of the dark that has enveloped her life after her husband's suicide. Testifying before a House Veterans Affairs Committee in July 2005, she said, "I thought we were just having marital problems. The first time

I heard anything about PTSD . . . was when a private therapist diagnosed him, a week before his death."[38]

The Defense Department's wall of silence regarding post-combat PTSD is currently being torn down brick-by-brick by the work of military family members like Pelkey, as well as Kevin and Joyce Lucey, whose son Jeffrey committed suicide five months before Michael Pelkey. "In the preparation for war," the Lucey's ask, "why was the healthcare system for our returning troops basically ignored?"[39]

Sarah Farmer, whose former fiancée Jeffrey Lehner killed himself and his father after losing his battle with PTSD, has been also working to make a difference by forming the Lehner Foundation. The cornerstone of this project is the Jeffrey House (www.lehner-foundation.org) where veterans will be able to access intensive PTSD treatment in a safe and secure environment.

Non-military types are also getting involved. One of the most committed is Dr. Robert Roerich, an expert in trauma therapy and PTSD and Vice President of the National Gulf War Resource Center. In his local Ohio community, he has teamed with military wife Darla Hough and the American Legion to offer a monthly program for returning veterans. Nationally, he mans a number of online PTSD help boards, sharing his expertise with those in need. He also works behind-the-scenes to bring people together on issues of PTSD education.

However, in order to bring sustained attention to the crisis that is occurring among our returning troops who suffer from PTSD, Stephanie Pelkey, Kevin and Joyce Lucey, Sarah Farmer and Dr. Robert Roerich and all the rest who are involved desperately need the rest of us to speak up. "The people of this nation have been far too quiet—their silence is deafening," say the Luceys. They ask that we stand with them to demand accountability from our leaders, and even more importantly, that we become active in giving our support to those who, after serving their country, return home afflicted with PTSD. The Luceys ask that "the people demand that their elected officials stop the talk and actually take action so that lives can be saved and the quality of life for our returning men and women can be improved." It is now time for the rest of us to join them and help tend to the work of caring for America's returning troops.

10. SETTING IT ALL INTO MOTION: RESOURCES FOR CONCERNED CITIZENS

"Never doubt that a small group of thoughtful, committed people can change the world. Indeed, it is the only thing that ever has."—Margaret Mead

It is my hope that after reading this book, you will be driven to get involved in order to help our soldiers who are suffering from combat-related PTSD. This chapter lists resources that anyone, from the merely curious to the most committed activist, can use. As the title of the book says, the goal is to "move a nation to care."

HOW TO GET STARTED

Learn about the experience of war by:

- Renting documentaries such as *The War Tapes, The Ground Truth, When I Came Home, The Sandstorm, Hidden Wounds, Why We Fight, After the Fog, Gunner Palace, Baghdad ER* or *Control Room.*
- Reading first-hand accounts of soldiers in combat, such as *Chasing Ghosts* by Paul Rieckhoff, *The Last True Story I'll Ever Tell* by John Crawford, *One Bullet Away* by Nathaniel

Fick, *In Conflict* by Yvonne Latty and *What Was Asked of Us* by Trish Wood.

- Googling words like "Iraq" or "veterans," or "combat ptsd" in order to keep abreast of the latest news and information.
- Joining a veterans' organization.

HOW TO COMMUNICATE WITH RETURNING VETERANS

- Welcome them home, and tell them you are glad they are back.
- Realize that they have had a unique experience that only those who have been to war can fully understand.
- Offer your support without pushing them to talk about their combat experiences.
- Use good judgment when offering your opinions on the war, appreciating the fact that the troops remain the sole conveyers of the truth. Watch those "hidden" judgments. Don't say to a returning parent, for example, "Oh, I couldn't have left my kids like that." They didn't have a choice.
- When communicating with someone coping with PTSD, use a soft touch.

HOW TO GET INVOLVED POLITICALLY

While government creeps along at its own slow pace, and our elected officials seem to be better at reacting than acting, a united public effort can give leaders the cover, and consequently the will, to do what is necessary. In order to play your part, please contact your senators and representatives at http://www.congress.org/congressorg/directory/congdir.tt.

Another good way for concerned citizens to get involved is by supporting the Joshua Omvig Veterans Suicide Prevention Act. This bill charges the VA with setting up a program to screen and monitor returning combat troops for risk of suicide. Introduced in the House by Representative Leonard Boswell, Democrat from Iowa, the bill is named after a 22-year-old Army Reserve soldier who committed suicide three days before Christmas 2005 after hearing that one of his fellow soldiers had been killed in action. You can visit the Joshua Omvig memorial at http://joshua-omvig. memory-of.com.

SPECIFIC LEGISLATION TO CONTACT YOUR ELECTED OFFICIALS ABOUT:

- **Lane Evans Veterans Health and Benefits Improvement Act of 2007 (S 117)**—This comprehensive bill would improve programs for the identification and treatment of post-deployment mental health conditions, including PTSD.
- **Joshua Omvig Veterans Suicide Prevention Act (S 479)**—Charges the Secretary of Veterans Affairs to develop and implement a comprehensive program for reducing the incidence of suicide among veterans.
- **Returning Servicemember VA Healthcare Insurance Act of 2007 (HR 612)**—Extends the health care for combat service in the Persian Gulf War or future hostilities from two years to five years after discharge or release.
- **Psychological Kevlar Act**—Directs the Secretary of Defense to develop and implement a plan of preventive and early-intervention measures, practices and procedures that reduce the likelihood that personnel in combat will develop PTSD or other stress-related injuries.

SPECIFIC POINTS TO LOBBY YOUR ELECTED OFFICIALS ABOUT:

- **Proper funding of the Veterans Administration.** The annual underfunding of the VA is a national disgrace.
- **Making VA funding mandatory, like Social Security.** No more scrounging around every year looking for budget scraps.

- **Reduction in the maximum tour length to six months.** A year (or more) is too long to fight.
- **Decreasing the number of combat deployments.** With each successive deployment, susceptibility to PTSD increases. No one should be deployed into a combat zone four or five times.
- **Forcing the DOD to follow its own regulations.** No PTSD-diagnosed troops should be redeployed into a combat zone.
- **Improving post-deployment assessments.** Make sure that all service members who need help receive it. Move away from relying on questionnaires and make physicals and one-on-one demob consultations mandatory again.
- **Investing more in counseling and support.** Rather than relying on quick-fix medications to solve psychological problems, invest time and resources in holistic wellness programs to help veterans and their families recover from the experience of war.
- **Removing the stigma for troops who seek help with their PTSD symptoms.** One of the easiest ways to do this would be to operate under the assumption that everyone will need some form of support following combat. Move away from a system where those struggling with PTSD must come forward on their own.
- **Requiring completion of a "boot camp in reverse" transitional training program.** Military families who have lost loved ones to suicide believe that there should be a more formal reentry program following return from combat.
- **Paying special attention to National Guard and Reserve forces.** Not being a part of a cohesive unit, they are especially susceptible to PTSD.

- **Extending health insurance coverage for the National Guard and Reserve service members to three years.** PTSD does not always show up in the first 180 days following combat duty.
- **Stop the closing of VA Hospitals and Veterans' Centers.** We should be providing more opportunities for veterans to access the benefits they have earned.
- **Increasing funding to community service boards.** Many troops—especially those with the National Guard and Reserve—do not have easy access to health services. Make sure that they have alternatives to getting the care they need, or else fully reimburse them for their private health care bills.
- **Increasing program offerings at Veteran's Centers.** Offer more complimentary group and individual classes that explain what PTSD is, how it can be treated and how to move beyond it and live a normal life.
- **Providing complimentary counseling to all immediate family members.** If the service member refuses to seek help, their spouse and children should have access to counseling services to help them through their loved one's reintegration process.
- **Increasing personal data security and treatment anonymity.** Many veterans will not come forward to get the help they need because they worry it may come back to haunt them when they're up for a job, etc.
- **Demanding that the DOD and VA do a better job of informing veterans of their rights.** Many veterans are unsure of what benefits they have earned and what rights they have coming to them.
- **Creating a free standing, confidential toll-free PTSD hotline.** Staffed 24 hours a day by professionals, and devoted fully to veterans coping with PTSD.

- **Improving the VA claims process.** Veterans who have health care needs do not have the time or energy to devote to lengthy and redundant forms, and do not have time to wait months for a decision on their claim.
- **Increasing the understanding of 21st century asymmetrical warfare.** The DOD should continue to make adjustments in its training to give service members the tools they need to counter the modern battlefield's unique stressors.

MAKING IT PERSONAL

While every individual has the power to exact change, often times we simply do not know where to start, or worry that our efforts will be squandered, or simply, that the problem is too large to fix. To counteract these concerns, reach out to one or two veterans in your local community, and tailor your volunteer efforts to your own personality, profession or skill set.

SAMPLE VOLUNTEER IDEAS

- **Writers:** Write articles about PTSD and send them to national and local newspapers and magazines. Pen letters to the editor.
- **Entertainers:** Arrange a concert or show, and donate the proceeds to a veterans' charity.
- **Construction workers:** Donate a weekend to an organization which builds complimentary homes for wounded soldiers.
- **Social workers or counselors:** Contact your local VA and ask if you can donate your time. Even a couple of days a month will make a difference. If you are in private practice, see about offering your services pro bono to returning vets and their families.
- **Firemen and police officers:** Organize events like a neighborhood BBQ or softball tournament in honor of the

troops. You are natural allies to our returning veterans.

- **Vietnam (or other) veterans:** Approach organizations like the American Legion and ask to use their space to host monthly meetings or gatherings. Continue to share your experiences and extend yourself to your newest brothers and sisters.
- **Artists:** Donate time at the VA teaching therapeutic art classes, which have been shown to help many cope with PTSD.
- **Frequent Flyers:** Donate your extra miles to Operation Hero Miles (http://www.heromiles.org) and make it possible for troops to fly home on leave for free.

SELECTED RESOURCES FOR RETURNING TROOPS AND THEIR FAMILIES

For a master list of organizations that assist returning combat veterans, go to America Supports You (www.americasupportsyou. mil/americasupportsyou/help.html).

REINTEGRATION/PTSD INFORMATION AND ASSISTANCE

Colorado Psychological Association

http://www.coloradopsych.org

The Support Our Family in Arms (SOFA) program provides a statewide network of volunteer mental health providers offering complimentary counseling services to OEF/OIF National Guard and Reserve veterans and their families. Phone: (303) 692-9303

Deep Streams

www.deepstreams.org/cominghome

Offers San Francisco Bay-area OEF/OIF veterans and their families a complimentary multi-disciplinary program that integrates psychological, meditative and expressive arts approaches to healing from war.

Employer Support of the Guard and Reserve (ESGR)

www.esgr.org/toolkit.asp

Online resources to assist with the special needs of Guard and Reserve forces.

Hearts Toward Home International

www.heartstowardhome.com

A non-profit that provides support, counseling, training, educational classes, materials, and reintegration and readjustment workshop/forums for military personnel (both active duty and veterans) and their families after wartime service.

National Alliance for the Mentally Ill

www.nami.org

Find a mental health services provider in your area.

Phone: 800-950-6264

National Institute of Mental Health

www.nimh.nih.gov/healthinformation/ptsdmenu.cfm

General PTSD information and links to booklets and databases

National Mental Health Association

www.nmha.org

Offers support groups, rehabilitation, socialization, and housing services through 340 community organizations across the country.

Phone: 800-969-6642 or 800-969-NMHA

ONE Freedom, Inc.

www.onefreedom.org

Complimentary reintegration programs and education resources for returning veterans with a focus on rebalancing the central

nervous system, regulating emotions and thought, and discharging stress from the body.
Phone: 888-443-VETS

Operation Comfort

www.operationcomfort.com/therapists.php
A nationwide network of 450 mental health providers and agencies providing services, free of charge, to veterans and family members who have a loved one serving in the Middle East.
Phone: 866-632-7868

The Returning Veterans Project NW

www.returningveterans.com
Offers free and confidential counseling to Portland-area veterans and their families of past and current Iraq and Afghanistan campaigns.
Phone: 503-402-1717 Email: info@returningveterans.com

Screening for Mental Health

https://www.militarymentalhealth.org/welcome.asp
Free and confidential online mental health self-assessment exam

Sidran Institute

www.sidran.org/survivor.html
Articles and help with finding a private therapist in your area

Soldier's Heart

www.soldiersheart.net
A national network of community-based, clinical consultations, veterans' return retreats, support groups and menor programs founded by the author, Edward Tick, M.D., of *War and Soul*.
Phone: 518-463-0588

The Soldiers Project

www.thesoldiersproject.org
Free, confidential psychological counseling for southern California
OEF/OIF vets and their families. Phone: 818-761-7438
Email: info@thesoldiersproject.org

Strategic Outreach to Families of All Reservists (SOFAR)

www.sofarusa.org
Complimentary psychotherapy and psycho-educational services for
New England-area families of Reservists and National Guard members stationed in or returning from Afghanistan, Iraq and Kuwait.

Valley Forge Return to Honor Workshops

www.returntohonorworkshop.com
Offers complimentary three-day intensive cognitive and experiential reintegration workshops, after theatre (after trauma) decompression training, and family integration programs for returning
Iraq and Afghanistan veterans and their families.

Veteran Love

www.veteranlove.com
Assisting wounded and disabled service men and women with
their post-war transition, this nonprofit has established a monthly
"emergency assistance" fund granting financial help to selected
veterans or military family members. Their online chat board is a
great resource.

Vets 4 Vets

www.vets4vets.us
Outreach to Iraq-era vets by Iraq-era vets, with support groups
located throughout the United States.
Phone: 520-250-0509

WebMD

www.webmd.com/hw/mental_health/hw184190.asp
The online A-Z Health Guide for PTSD offers a brief overview.

GOVERNMENT REINTEGRATION/PTSD ASSISTANCE AND INFORMATION

Deployment Health Clinical Center
www.pdhealth.mil/op_stress.asp
DoD's combat and operational stress information page.

DoD Force Health Protection & Readiness Programs

http://deploymenthealthlibrary.fhp.osd.mil
The Deployment Health and Family Readiness Library is an
enormous collection of government deployment and reintegration
information and resources.

Military OneSource

www.militaryonesource.com
Provided by the Department of Defense at no cost to active duty,
Guard and Reserve (regardless of activation status) and their
families, services include help with child care, personal finances,
emotional support during deployments, relocation information, or
resources needed for special circumstances. Their website is filled
with resources, but services are also available by phone and face-
to-face through private counseling sessions in the local
community.
Stateside: CONUS: 800-342-9647
Overseas: OCONUS Universal Free Phone: 800-3429-6477
Collect from Overseas: OCONUS Collect: 484-530-5908

My HealtheVet (MHV)

www.myhealth.va.gov
The VA's gateway to veteran health benefits and services.

National Center for Post-Traumatic Stress Disorder
www.ncptsd.org
Part of the VA, this website offers fact sheets and helpful guides
(like *The Iraq War Clinician Guide, 2nd Edition*, and *Returning
from the War Zone: A Guide for Families*), videos, medical papers,
and other PTSD-related info for veterans, mental health care
providers, researchers and the general public.

VA Facilities & Locator Directory
www1.va.gov/directory/guide/home.asp?isFlash=1

VA Seamless Transition
www.seamlesstransition.va.gov
Complete benefit information for returning Active Duty, National
Guard and Reserve service members of Operations Enduring
Freedom and Iraqi Freedom.

Vet Center Readjustment Counseling Services
www.va.gov/rcs/

War-Related Illness and Injury Study Centers (WRIISC)
www.wri.med.va.gov/index.html
This WRIISC in East Orange, New Jersey, offers free assessments
to OEF/OIF vets of deployment-related persistent fatigue, pain,
cognitive and sleep problems. U.S. veterans deployed to hostile
areas and with deployment related health concerns and/or symptoms are eligible for a free, individualized WRIISC evaluation.
Phone: 800-248-8005

VETERANS ORGANIZATIONS
Iraq and Afghanistan Veterans of America (IAVA)
www.iava.org/index.php

Nation's first and largest group dedicated to the troops and veterans of the wars in Iraq and Afghanistan, and their civilian supporters.

Military Families Speak Out (MFSO)

www.mfso.org
Active national organization of over 3,100 families opposed to war in Iraq who have relatives or loved ones in the military.
Phone: 617-983-0710

National Gulf War Resource Center (NGWRC)

www.ngwrc.org
Leading international organization providing advocacy for Gulf War veterans. Phone: 816-531-7183 Toll-free: 866-531-7183

Veterans for America (VFA)

www.veteransforamerica.org
Address the causes, conduct and consequences of war. Excellent database of articles and resource guide. Phone: 202-483-9222

Veterans for Peace (VFP)

www.veteransforpeace.org
Having 135 nationwide chapters, and dozens of international affiliations, VRP is an educational and humanitarian organization committed to finding peaceful solutions to war.
Phone: 314-725-6005

SUPPORT RESOURCES
American Gulf War Veterans Association
www.gulfwarvets.com/ubb/ultimatebb.php

MSN Groups

http://groups.msn.com/AftermathofwarcopingwithPTSD too
Aftermath of War: Coping with PTSD forum and resources

Yahoo Groups

http://health.groups.yahoo.com/group/SLOOMS/
SLOOMS - Support Loved Ones of Military Suicides - is
manned by the Joshua Omvig family and offers support and community to all military families and veterans.

Befrienders Worldwide

www.befrienders.org
Toll-free confidential help. Additional helpline numbers and
resources at website, many of them available in a variety of
languages.
Phone: 800-365-4044 or 800-893-9900

Focus on Recovery

24/7 national alcohol and drug abuse addiction and treatment
hotline.
Phone: 800-374-2800 or 800-234-1253

Kristin Brooks Hope Center

www.hopeline.com
Confidential 24/7 help via the National Hopeline Network.
Phone: 800-784-2433 or 800-SUICIDE

Miles Foundation

Domestic violence help. Phone: 877-570-0688

Military OneSource

www.militaryonesource.com
DoD contracted helpline (24/7)
Phone: 800-342-9647 in U.S.
Phone: 800-3429-6477 outside of U.S.

National Coalition for Homeless Vets

www.nchv.org/standdown.cfm
Visit online to find shelter locations and veteran Stand Down days (one to three days of community-provided access to food, clothing, medical, legal and mental health assistance, job counseling and referral, and most importantly, companionship and camaraderie for homeless veterans) scheduled across the country.
Phone: 800-838-4357 or 800-VET-HELP

National Veterans Foundation Help Line

www.nvf.org
Offers emotional support, a listening ear, and information about veteran services and resources available in your community and throughout the United States. This is a non-profit organization, not affiliated with the government.
Phone: 888-777-4443 Email: vetsupport@nvf.org

The Samaritans

www.metanoia.org/suicide/samaritans.htm
Provides confidential emotional support to any person, who is suicidal or despairing.
Email: jo@samaritans.org

Suicide Prevention Action Network USA

www.spanusa.org Phone: 888-649-1366

Veterans of the Vietnam War (VVnW)

www.theveteranscoalition.org

Comprised of ninety posts worldwide, their many programs maintain, improve, preserve and defend the quality of life of all veterans and their families. 24/7 helpline.

Phone: 800-843-8626 or 800-VIETNAM

VA CLAIMS FILING HELP

Hadit

www.hadit.com

Tips and help with filing VA and SSA claims. Handy veterans benefits timetable.

http://www.hadit.com/veteransbenefitstimetable.pdf.

Infinity Publishing

www.ptsdmanual.com

Military Veterans PTSD Reference Manual, a comprehensive online book covering the history and treatment of combat PTSD as well as detailed information on the VA medical claims process.

National Association of County Service Officers (NACVSO)

www.nacvso.org

Recognized officially by the U.S. Department of Veterans Affairs "for the purpose of preparation, presentation, and prosecution of claims under laws administered by the Department of Veterans Affairs." Go to their website to find an office nearest you to assist with your claim filing.

National Organization of Veterans Advocates (NOVA)

www.vetadvocates.com

A non-profit organization of attorneys and practitioners who practice before the U.S. Court of Appeals for Veterans Claims

(CAVC). Call 800-810-8387 to arrange an attorney to represent you; pro bono assistance available through the Veterans Pro Bono Consortium.

PTSD Help Network
www.ptsdhelp.net/id18.html
Print and fill out this PTSD Benefit Claims Worksheet as soon as you can; it will save you time and frustration as you fill out your required VA forms.

U.S. Armed Forces Legal Assistance Locater
http://legalassistance.law.af.mil/content/locator.php
Part of the DOD, an online search form to help you find a legal assistance office near you.

VA Regional Office (VARO)
At the first sign of a problem, call to find the nearest VARO. Then write a letter to the VA (this will be your informal claim) to let them know you are planning to access your benefits. After this first notification, you may then proceed to fill out the required formal application, VA form 21-526.
Phone: 800-827-1000

VA Watchdog
www.vawatchdog.org/how%20to%20file%20a%20claim.htm
Advice from veterans on filing your VA claim

Veterans Advocate Service Officer
http://www.vfw.org/resources/vetservices/serofficerjan2006.pdf
To receive help with discharge upgrades, seeking benefits, or filing a VA claim, call 800-562-2308 to find an officer located near you or check the Veterans of Foreign Wars Service Officers Directory.

Vietnam Veterans of America
www.vva.org/Benefits/ptsd.htm
PTSD Benefits Guide for filing VA claims.

Widener University School of Law
www.law.widener.edu/academics/clinics_externships/de_veterans.shtml
Delaware Volunteer Legal Services (DVLS) offers free legal aid to veterans subsisting at 125 percent of the poverty level who have been denied benefits by the Regional Office and the Board of Veterans Appeals and wish to take an appeal to Court of Veterans Appeals (COVA).

FREE ONLINE BOOKLETS AND VIDEOS
American Psychiatric Association
www.healthyminds.org/multimedia/ptsd.pdf
Let's Talk Facts PTSD brochure

My work with ePluribus Media continues on the PTSD Timeline. If you know of an incident, please email timelines@epluribusmedia.org.

ACKNOWLEDGEMENTS

Moving a Nation to Care is a brief portrait of a story that is still being written. My greatest thanks to the military families and returning troops that have shared their time, experience, expertise and personal accounts during the writing of this book: Stefanie Pelkey, Joyce and Kevin Lucey, Thomas Doherty, Patrick Doherty, Sarah Farmer, Laura Kent, the family of Joshua Omvig, Jim Starowicz, Zack Bazzi, Paul Rieckhoff, Abbie Pickett, Perry Jefferies, Steve Robinson, Jonathon Powers, Charles Sheehan-Miles, Eric Massa, Wade Hampton Fulmer, Mike Meagher, Dick Pierce, John Laesch, Peter Laesch, Michael Bailey, Bruce Jacobsen, Dale Peters, Mark Fleming, Dennis Stout and John Henry.

To Robert "Doc" Roerich, M.D., and Penny Coleman go my warmest thanks. You've inspired and sustained me as you surely do others. I am deeply honored to have had the chance to work with you, to learn from you, and to benefit from the many kind words and actions you have sent in my direction. Additional appreciation goes to Dr. Edward Tick, Dr. Rachel MacNair, Trish Wood, Taryn Roeder, Rick Anderson, Reese Butler, Michael Fancher, Lisa Chedekel, Matthew Kauffman, Bryan Bender, Pamela Martineau, Kay Berenson, Taylor Marsh, Mark Boal, Aldon Hynes, Mark Karlin, Jeanine Plant, Elena Lesley, Alex Urevick-Ackelsberg, Simon at *Power and Control* and Hsien-Hsien Lei at *Genetics and*

Health. And a special nod to the producers, director, cast and crew of *The War Tapes*.

Thank you to the vibrant online communities and veterans organizations who offer the support and feedback loop a writer on this topic can only wish for: Veterans for America, Iraq and Afghanistan Veterans of America, National Gulf War Resource Center, General Wesley Clark's Community Network, Veterans for Peace, Veteran Love, Military Families Speak Out, VietNow, everyone involved with UMass' Media Giraffe Project (most especially Bill Densmore), SoapBlox/Chicago, Daily Kos, My Left Wing, Political Cortex, Booman Tribune, Blue Force, and TPM Cafe. Singular thanks to RubDMC, Maryscott O'Connor, Barb Morrill, Melvin, Eugene, Occams Hatchet, Mark in SFO, Tom Ball, Steve Aldrich, Sinister Rae, Martha, Carol and all of my friends at CCN.

To my ePluribusMedia mentors and colleagues: You are a citizen journalist's best friend. My success is directly linked to the ideas, leads, advice, moral support, editing, fact-checking, friendship and dozens of other resources and opportunities you have given me. An enormous amount of appreciation goes to JeninRI, literally responsible for the PTSD Timeline's existence (along with programmer extraordinaire LeftyLimblog), and the driving force behind the fact-checking of every incident in its database. To D.E. Ford, MSW and retired Naval Commander Jeff Huber: thank you for scooping me up and letting me work with two pros. Thanks to everyone behind the scenes, too: standingup, kfred, Aaron Barlow, Barbara J. Schulz, radish, Roxy, Susie Dow, Kay Shepherd, Andrew Brenner, Timothy D. Smith, Greyhawk, luaptifer, Todd Johnson, Welshman, Chris White, intranets, rba, clammyc and the rest of the gifted gang at ePluribus Media.

A special word of thanks to Cho. Our ePMedia collaborations, your solid professional advice and kind personal mentorship coupled with the sheer power to move mountains when it comes to making a deadline are a thing of beauty.

To my publishers, Robert Lasner and Elizabeth Clementson: thank you for making this dialogue with the American people possible. Your patience with me during my blocks will be long remembered and appreciated.

To my imprintink.com family: A world of appreciation to clients and friends whose websites have had to make generous allowances for my absence this past year. The fabulous Jeanne Coe and the whole gang at Art Corporation; John Karian at Wetland Splendors; Paul Youngblood at Snappy Sauce Company; and especially cousin, client, and friend Monika Oroszlán and husband, Csaba, of Oak Photography and SYNCOM Consulting respectively.

To the rest of my family and friends: never has anyone had a more interesting and special group of people to draw from. My parents, Zsuzsanna and Géza have had their lives directly touched by overpowering global events, and their stories and experiences have enriched my life. My love extends to them and to my late sister Zsuzsanna and sister Eva, their husbands Terry and Bryan, and my nieces and nephew Molly, Liam and Ilona. You have filled me with happiness and pride, and I love you all. The same feelings of love and gratitude to my extended family: the best in-laws around, Shirley, and my late father-in-law Edward (a former World War II veteran of the Pacific theater); my brothers- and sisters in law Robin and Ed, Mike, Patty and Frank, Tim and Lynn; and nieces and nephews Frank, August, Peter, Molly, Sam, Chris, Sophie and Audrey.

And to the man I am blessed to call my best friend and husband, Tom: thank you, sweetheart. You saw the good, the bad, and the ugly of the writing process, and helped me to get through the many days and nights of work on this project. This book is yours as much as mine.

Finally, to our returning troops: know that some of us civilians are interested in hearing your stories and at the ready to do whatever you need us to do to ensure that your transistion to the homefront is successful. Keep talking to us, and keep telling us what you need. We're ready to listen, and above all, we're ready to welcome you home.

One final, special thanks to James Blake Miller. I hope this book is one small measure of the gratitude you deserve for your work to educate the American public on the plight of today's returning military veterans. You are a valiant and humble protagonist who has served his country well both in and out of uniform. I hope you have found the peace that you fought for and so rightly deserve. You and your peers have the nation's gratitude.

SELECTED BIBLIOGRAPHY

Agnew, James B., Clifton R. Franks, William R. Griffiths. *The Great War*. West Point: United States Military Academy Department of History, 1984.

Alley, Lee with Wade Stevenson. *Back from War: A Quest for Life After Death*. Midlothian, VA: Exceptional Publishing, 2006)

Armstrong, Keith, LCSW, Suzanne Best, PhD, and Paula Domenici, PhD. *Courage After Fire: Coping Strategies for Troops Returning from Iraq and Afghanistan and Their Families*. Berkeley: Ulysses Press, 2006.

Bacevich, Andrew J. *The New American Militarism: How Americans Are Seduced by War*. New York: Oxford University Press, 2005.

Bodansky, Yossef. *The Secret History of the Iraq War*. New York: Regan Books, 2004.

Brokaw, Tom. *The Greatest Generation*. New York: Random House, 1998.

Cantrell, Bridget C., PhD. and Chuck Dean. *Down Range to Iraq and Back*. Seattle: WordSmith Publishing, 2005.

Coleman, Penny. *Flashback: Posttraumatic Stress Disorder, Suicide, and the Lessons of War*. Boston: Beacon Press, 2006.

Crawford, John. *The Last True Story I'll Ever Tell: An Accidental Soldier's Account of the War in Iraq*. New York: Riverhead Books, 2005.

Cunningham, J. Baron, PhD. *The Stress Management Sourcebook: Everything You Need to Know*. 2nd ed. Los Angeles: Lowell House, 2000.

D'Este, Carlo. *Patton: A Genius for War*. New York: Harper Collins, 1995.

Dean, Eric T., Jr. *Shook Over Hell: Post-Traumatic Stress, Vietnam, and the Civil War*. Cambridge: Harvard University Press, 1997.

Edgerton, Robert B. *Like Lions They Fought: The Zulu War and the Last Black Empire in South Africa*. New York: Ballatine Books, 1988.

Exum, Andrew. *This Man's Army: A Soldier's Story from the Front Lines of the War on Terrorism*. New York: Gotham Books, 2004.

Friedman, Matthew J., MD, PhD. *Post-Traumatic Stress Disorder: The Latest Assessment and Treatment Strategies.* Kansas City: Compact Clinicals, 2003.

Garbriel, Richard A. *No More Heroes: Madness and Psychiatry in War.* New York: Hill and Wang, 1987.

Gibson, James William. *Warrior Dreams: Violence and Manhood in Post-Vietnam America.* New York: Hill and Wang, 1994.

Glassner, Ronald J., MD. *Wounded: Vietnam to Iraq.* New York: George Braziller, 2006.

Goldman, Peter and Tony Fuller. *Charlie Company: What Vietnam Did to Us.* New York: Quill, 1983.

Grossman, Dave. *On Killing: The Psychological Cost of Learning to Kill in War and Society.* New York: Back Bay Books, 1995.

Grossman, Dave with Loren W. Christensen. *On Combat: The Psychology and Physiology of Deadly Conflict in War and in Peace.* Belleville: PPCT Research Publications, 2004.

Hart, Ashley B., II, PhD. *An Operators Manual for Combat PTSD: Essays for Coping.* San Jose: Writer's Showcase, 2000.

Hedges, Chris. *War is a Force That Gives Us Meaning.* New York: Anchor Books, 2002.

———. *What Every Person Should Know About War.* New York: Free Press, 2003.

Henderson, Kristin. *While They're at War: The True Story of American Families on the Homefront.* New York: Houghton Mifflin Company, 2006.

Hitchcock, F. C. *Stand To: A Diary of the Trenches, 1915–1918. 1937.* Dallington, Heathfield: The Naval & Military Press, 2001.

Jones, Edgar and Simon Wessely. *Shell Sock to PTSD: Military Psychiatry from 1900 to the Gulf War.* New York: Psychology Press, 2005.

Jones, F., L. Sparacino, and V. Wilcox, eds. "Combat Stress." *Textbook of Military Medicine: Vol. 6.* Washington, DC: Office of the Surgeon General, US Army, 1995.

Karnow, Stanley. *Vietnam: A History.* New York: Viking Press, 1983.

Kearney, George E., Mark Creamer, Rick Marshall, and Anne Goyne, eds. *Military Stress and Performance: The Australian Defence Force Experience.* Melbourne: Melbourne University Press, 2003.

Kennedy, David M. *Freedom from Fear: The American People in Depression and War, 1929–1945.* New York: Oxford University Press, 1999.

Latty, Yvonne. *In Conflict: Iraq War Veterans Speak Out on Duty, Loss, and the Fight to Stay Alive.* Sausalito, CA: PoliPointPress, 2006.

Livington, Gary. *Fallujah, With Honor: First Battalion, Eight Marine's Role in Operation Phantom Fury.* North Topsail Beach, NC: Caisson Press, 2006.

MacNair, Rachel M.D. *Perpetration-Induced Traumatic Stress: The Psychological*

Consequences of Killing (Psychological Dimensions to War and Peace). Westport, CT: Praeger Publishers, 2002.

McKibben, Bill. *The Age of Missing Information*. New York: Plume, 1992.

Miller, Robert J. with Stephen J. Hrycyniak. *Grief Quest: Reflections for Men Coping With Loss*. St. Meinrad: One Caring Place, 1989.

Nadelson, Theodore, MA, MD. *Trained to Kill: Soldiers at War*. Baltimore: John Hopkins University Press, 2005.

Nicosia, Gerald. *Home to War: A History of the Vietnam Veterans' Movement*. New York: Carroll & Graf Publishers, 2001.

Pavlicin, Karen M. *Surviving Deployment: A Guide for Military Families*. St. Paul: Elva Resa Publishing, 2003.

Province, Charles M. *The Unknown Patton*. New York: Hippocrene Books, 1983.

Reynolds, Clark G. *America at War 1941–1945: The Home Front*. New York: Gallery Books, 1990.

Rieckhoff, Paul. *Chasing Ghosts: A Soldier's Fight for America from Baghdad to Washington*. New York: New American Library, 2006.

Ricks, Thomas E., *Fiasco: The American Military Adventure in Iraq*. New York: The Penguin Press, 2006.

Roth-Douquet, Kathy and Frank Schaeffer. *AWOL: The Unexcused Absence of America's Upper Classes from Military Service—and How It Hurts Our Country*. New York: HaperCollins, 2006.

Schmookler, Andrew Bard. *Out of Weakness: Healing the Wounds That Drive Us to War*. New York: Bantam Books, 1988.

Scott, Wilbur J., *Vietnam Veterans Since the War: The Politics of Ptsd, Agent Orange, and the National Memorial*. University of Oklahoma Press, 2004.

Shay, Jonathan, MD, PhD. *Achilles in Vietnam: Combat Trauma and the Undoing of Character*. New York: Scribner, 1994.

Shephard, Ben. *A War of Nerves: Soldiers and Psychiatrists in the Twentieth Century*. Cambridge: Harvard University Press, 2001.

Siddle, Bruce K. *Sharpening the Warrior's Edge: The Psychology & Science of Training*. Belleville: PPCT Research Publicans, 1995.

Tick, Edward, Ph.D. *War and the Soul: Healing Our Nation's Veterans from Post-traumatic Stress Disorder*. Wheaton: Quest Books, 2005.

Van der Kolk, Bessel A., Alexander C. McFarlane, and Lars Weisaeth, eds. *Traumatic Stress: The Effects of Overwhelming Experience on Mind, Body, and Society*. New York: The Guilford Press, 1996.

Walzer, Michael. *Just and Unjust Wars: A Moral Argument with Historical Illustrations*. New York: Basic Books., 1977.

Wood, Trish. *What Was Asked of Us: An Oral History of the Iraq War by the Soldiers Who Fought It*. New York: Little, Brown and Company, 2006.

Zajtchuk, Russ, MC, US Army, and Ronald F. Bellamy, MC, US Army, eds. *Textbook of Military Medicine*. Washington, DC: Office of the Surgeon General, Department of the Army, 1995.

Zinn, Howard. *A People's History of the United States*. New York: Harper Colophon.

NOTES

PREFACE

1. "Voices From the Front: Vets In Their Own Words," *City Belt*, July 17, 2006, http://citybelt.typepad.com/citybelt/2006/07/voices_from_the.html.

2. Scott Shane, "Data Suggests Vast Costs Loom in Disability Claims," *New York Times*, October 11, 2006, A18.

3. Kevin G. Hall and David Montgomery, "Official Iraq war costs don't tell the whole story," *McClatchy Newspapers*, December 5, 2006; Leo Shane III, "Number of veterans seeking treatment for stress has doubled," *Stars & Stripes*, November 2, 2006, http://www.estripes.com/article.asp?section=104&article=40227&archive=true.

4. The National Security Archive, "VA Takes Nine Months to Locate Data on Disability Claims by Veterans of the Iraq and Afghanistan Wars," October 10, 2006, http://www.gwu.edu/%7Ensarchiv/news/20061010/index.htm.

5. Rick Anderson, "Home Front Casualties," *Seattle Weekly*, August 31, 2005, http://www.seattleweekly.com/news/0535/050831_news_soldiers.php.

6. U.S. Department of Veterans Affairs: National Center for PTSD, "What is Posttraumatic Stress Disorder?," July 20, 2006 http://www.ncptsd.va.gov/facts/general/fs_what_is_ptsd.html.

7. Ibid.

8. Alison Walker-Baird, "Stress Wounds: Dealing with the Mental Scars of War," *Frederick Post*, November 13, 2006.

9. "PTSD Care Demand Taxing System," *Bangor Daily News*, June 21, 2006; Donna St. George, "Mental Health Services Questioned," *Washington Post*, August 20, 2006, http://www.washingtonpost.com/wp-dyn/content/article/2006/08/19/AR2006081900570.html; Leo Shane III, "Number of veterans seeking treatment

for stress has doubled," *Stars and Stripes*, November 2, 2006; Kevin G. Hall and David Montgomery, "Official Iraq war costs don't tell the whole story," *McClatchy Newspapers*, December 5, 2006.

10. Charles W. Hoge, M.D., Carl A. Castro, Ph.D., Stephen C. Messer, Ph.D., Dennis McGurk, Ph.D., Dave I. Cotting, Ph.D., and Robert L. Koffman, M.D., M.P.H, "Combat Duty in Iraq and Afghanistan, Mental Health Problems, and Barriers to Care," *New England Journal of Medicine*, 351 (July 2004): 13–22.

11. National Geographic-Roper 2006, "Survey of Geographic Literarcy," http://www9.nationalgeographic.com/roper2006/findings.html

12. Judith Coburn, "Caring for Veterans on the Cheap," *Tom's Dispatch*, April 27, 2006, http://www.tomdispatch.com/index.mhtml?pid=80291.

13. Lisa Bilmes and Joseph Stiglitz, "Encore Review," *Milken Institute Review*, (December 2006), http://www.milkeninstitute.org/publications/review/2006_12/76_83mr32.pdf

14. Amvets, "*Amvets Symposium Report: Voices for Action, A Focus on the Changing Needs of America's Veterans,*" November 9, 2006, http://www.amvets.org/Assets/pdfs/Amvets_Symposium_Report_FINAL.pdf

15. Mark Williams, "Supporting Our Troops Past and Present," *The Bulletin Online*, November 2006, http://www.thebulletin.com/archives/2006/november/veteransday2006.htm

16. Epluribus Media, "PTSD Timeline," http://timelines.epluribusmedia.org/timelines/index.php?&mjre=PTSD&table_name=tl_ptsd&function=search&order=date&order_type=ASC

PART I—A BACKWARDS GLANCE

1. In May 2006, as the *Moving a Nation to Care* project got underway, I attempted to get in touch with Miller. I felt his story the perfect one to open my dialogue with the American people, and I wanted to get his blessing. That same month, I received word (via the kindness of a mutual contact) from Miller agreeing to an interview for the book. He expressed his wishes about what the project might become, saying, "I'm interested only if it's going to be a positive outlook on PTSD and it is aimed at helping our veterans, and others, who have it. I want to tell the story, not for the sake of telling it, but to try and change how things are perceived and maybe to alter the labeling." As the writing picked up in the summer of 2006, the news of his separation from his wife led to a public plea by Miller for privacy. I respected his wishes. I hope, Blake, that you are pleased with the direction and mission of the final product; I did try to stay true to your desire to tell the tale in order to help and not hurt our troops and their families. James Blake Miller, "Re:

Request for interview for book by national journalist," Email to Robert Roerich MD, forwarded to author, May 22, 2006.

1. THE FACE OF WAR

1. Much of the detailed information regarding Fallujah and the 1-8's movements are gleaned from the following two exhaustive OPF accounts: Gary Livingston's *Fallujah, With Honor: First Battalion, Eight Marine's Role in Operation Phantom Fury,* (North Topsail Beach: Caisson Press, 2006) and the online series "Battle for Fallujah, our warfighters towered in maturity and guts," *Talking Proud! Magazine,* http://www.talkingproud.us/Military042805.html.

2. Gary Livington, *Fallujah, With Honor: First Battalion, Eight Marine's Role in Operation Phantom Fury,* 10.

3. Jim Warren, "Former Marine is 'Marlboro Man' no more," *Knight Ridder,* January 22, 2006.

4. Matthew Stannard, "The War Within," *San Francisco Chronicle,* January 29, 2006.

5. Ibid.

6. Jake Tapper, Roxanna Sherwood and Karin Weinberg, "'Marlboro Man' Marine Describes Struggle with PTSD," *ABC News,* April 13, 2006, http://abcnews.go.com/WNT/story?id=1838802&page=1.

7. Mike Needs, Public Editor, "Most look past the smoke, laud photo of weary Marine," *Akron Beacon Journal,* November 14, 2004, http://www.ohio.com/mld/ohio/news/10179027.htm?1c.

8. Normon Solomon, "Media's War Images Delude Instead of Inform," *Common Dreams,* January 9, 2006, http://www.commondreams.org/views06/0109-20.htm.

9. Ibid.

10. Patrick J. McDonnell, "Marine Whose Photo Lit Up Imaginations Keeps His Cool," *Los Angeles Times,* November 13, 2004.

11. Tapper, Sherwood, Weinberg, "'Marlboro Man' Marine Describes Struggle with PTSD."

12. Warren, "Former Marine is "Marlboro Man" no more."

13. David Zucchino, "Iconic Marine is Home but Not at Ease," *Los Angeles Times,* May 19, 2006.

14. McDonnell, "Marine Whose Photo Lit Up Imaginations Keeps His Cool."

15. "'Face of War' Speaks,"interview by Harry Miller,CBS The Early Show,February 8, 2005, http://www.cbsnews.com/stories/2005/02/07/earlyshow/main672157.shtml.

16. Ibid.

17. "'Marlboro Marine': Home Front Woes," *CBS The Early Show,* January 3, 2006, http://www.cbsnews.com/stories/2006/01/03/earlyshow/main1174711.shtml.

18. Warren, "Former Marine is "Marlboro Man" no more."

19. Stannard, "The War Within."

20. Ibid.

21. "'Marlboro Marine': Home Front Woes."

22. Tapper, Sherwood, Weinberg, "'Marlboro Man' Marine Describes Struggle with PTSD."

23. Warren, "Former Marine is "Marlboro Man" no more."

24. Zucchino, "Iconic Marine is Home but Not at Ease."

25. "'Marlboro Marine:' Home Front Woes."

26. Solomon, "Media's War Images Delude Instead of Inform."

27. Tapper, Sherwood, Weinberg "'Marlboro Man' Marine Describes Struggle with PTSD."

2. A BRIEF HISTORY OF PTSD

1. Ben Shephard, *A War of Nerves: Soldiers and Psychiatrists in the Twentieth Century*, (Cambridge: Harvard University Press, 2000), xxi.

2. Carlo D'Este, *Patton: A Genius for War*, (New York: HarperCollins, 1995), 533.

3. Charles M. Province, *The Unknown Patton* (New York: Hippocrene Books, 1983), http://pattonhq.com/unknown/chap08.html.

4. D'Este, *Patton: A Genius for War*, 533.

5. Ibid., 534.

6. Charles M. Province, *The Unknown Patton* (New York: Hippocrene Books, 1983), http://pattonhq.com/unknown/chap08.html.

7. D'Este, *Patton: A Genius for War*, 534.

8. Ibid., 536.

9. Ibid., 539.

10. Ibid., 538–540.

11. Steven Bentley, "A Short History of PTSD: From Thermopylae to Hue, Soldiers Have Always Had A Disturbing Reaction To War," *The VVA Veteran*, March/April 2005.

12. Ibid.

13. Major Stephane Grenier, "Operational Stress Injuries (OSI): A New Way to Look at an Old Problem," Canadian Forces Support Personal Agency: Director of Military Family Services, June 12, 2005, http://www.cfpsa.com/en/psp/dmfs/resources/osiss_e.asp

14. Franklin D. Jones, M.D., F.A.P.A, "Psychiatric Lessons of War," in *War Psychiatry*, The Textbooks of Military Medicine, ed. Brigadier General Russ Zajtchuk, M.C., (Washington, DC: Office of The Surgeon General, Department of the Army, 1995), 6.

15. Ibid, 8.

16. Nicolas L. Rock., M.D., F.A.P.A., James W. Stokes., M.D., Ronald J.Koshes, M.D., Joe Fagan M.D., William R.Cline, M.D., and Franklin D. Jones, M.D., F.A.P.A., "U.S. Army Combat Psychiatry," in *War Psychiatry*, The Textbooks of Military Medicine, ed. Brigadier General Russ Zajtchuk, M.C., (Washington, DC: Office of The Surgeon General, Department of the Army, 1995), 153.

17. Penny Coleman, *Flashback: Posttraumatic Stress Disorder, Suicide, and the Lessons of War*. (Boston: Beacon Press, 2006), 23–24.

18. "U.S. Army Combat Psychiatry," *War Psychiatry*, 153.

19. Ralph Harrington, "The Railway Accident: Trains, Trauma and Technological Crisis In Nineteenth Century Britain," in *Traumatic Pasts: History and Trauma in the Modern Age*, ed. Mark S. Micale and Paul Lerner, (Cambridge: Cambridge University Press, 2001), 31-57.

20. "U.S. Army Combat Psychiatry," *War Psychiatry*, 154.

21. F. C. Hitchcock. *Stand To: A Diary of the Trenches, 1915–1918*. (London: Hurst & Blackett, 1937; repr., Heathfield, England: The Naval & Military Press, Ltd., 2001).

22. "Psychiatric Lessons of War," *War Psychiatry*, 9.

23. Ibid.

24. Ibid, 11.

25. Paul Wanke, "American Military Psychiatry and Its Role Among Ground Forces in World War II," *The Journal of Military History* 63, no. 1 (January 1999): 127.

26. "Psychiatric Lessons of War," *War Psychiatry*, 11–12.

27. Ibid.

28. Peter J. Murphy, "The Stress of Deployment," *Military Stress and Performance: The Australian Defence Force Experience*, (Melbourne: Melbourne University Press, 2003), 7.

29. "Psychiatric Lessons of War," *War Psychiatry*, 16-17.

30. Ibid.

31. Ibid.

32. Kate Mulligan, "For PTSD Care, It's a Long Way from Vietnam to Iraq," *Psychiatric News* 39, no.9 (May 7, 2004): 1, http://pn.psychiatryonline.org/cgi/content/full/39/9/1

33. In years past, post-traumatic stress disorder has been referred to by any number of names and phrases including (in no particular order) PTSD, soldier's heart, exhausted heart, irritable heart, Da Costa's syndrome, Swiss disease, railway (or railroad) spine, railway shock, railway brain, fear neurosis, Erichsen's disease, hysteria, exhaustion, disorderly action of the heart, heimweh (German, 'homesickness'), war hysteria, traumatic hysteria, traumatic neurasthenia, shell

shock, battleshock, battle reaction, battle fatigue, battle neurosis, battle exhaustion, combat fatigue, combat stress reaction, combat-operational stress reaction, war neurosis, war syndrome, traumatic neurosis (of war), nostalgia, mind sickness, combat trauma, combat exhaustion, nerves, maladie du pays (French, 'disease of the country'), not yet diagnosed nervous, psychoneurosis, post-war disorder, acute stress disorder, acute stress reaction, gross stress reaction, post-Vietnam syndrome (PVS), post-combat disorder, catastrophic stress disorder, mental collapse, in-country effect, psychological injury, mental trauma, Old Sergeant Syndrome, acute combat reaction, acute combat stress reaction, neurocirculatory asthenia, effort syndrome, lack of moral fibre, estar roto (Spanish, 'to be broken'), delayed stress syndrome, psycho-neurosis, psychiatric collapse, Vietnam disease, nervous disease, nervous shock, physical shock, neurasthenia following shock and accident, accident neurosis, post-traumatic shock, veteran's chronic stress syndrome, explosion blow, cerebro-medullary shock, emotional disturbance, simple continued fever, cardiac muscular exhaustion, cerebro-spinal shock, wind contusions, posttraumatic illness, chronic multisymptom illness, disordered action of the heart, post-combat stress reaction, Vietnam veteran syndrome, buck fever, re-entry syndrome, and post-Viet Nam psychiatric syndrome (PVNPS).

34. Gerald Nicosia, *Home to War: A History of the Vietnam Veterans' Movement* (New York: Carroll & Graf Publishers, 2001), 158–159

35. The current criteria for PTSD in *DSM-IV* states that a person must be "exposed to a traumatic event" and confronted with "actual or threatened death or serious injury, or a threat to the physical integrity of self or others." Their response would have "involved intense fear, helplessness, or horror" at the time. PTSD requires that a month after the event they're still experiencing flashbacks, having nightmares, emotionally and/or physically responding to certain triggers, actively avoiding thoughts and feelings or discussions or people or places that remind them of the trauma, feeling 'pumped up' or not able to relax, getting angry easily, etc. All of these symptoms would combine in the patient, affecting their ability to function in social and employment situations.

36. Nicosia, *Home to War*, 179

37. Ann Scott Tyson, "Suicides in Marine Corps Rise by 29%," *Washington Post*, February, 25, 2005, http://www.washingtonpost.com/wp-dyn/articles/A51933-2005Feb24.html.

38. "Army Suicides Hit Highest Level Since 1993," *Associated Press*, April 21, 2006.

39. Bret A Moore and Greg M. Reger, "Combating Stress in Iraq," *Scientific American*, February/March 2006, 35.

40. Matthew J. Friedman, MD, PhD. *Post Traumatic Stress Disorder: The Latest*

Assessment and Treatment Strategies, (Kansas City, Missouri: Compact Clinicals, 2003), 1.

41. Bessel A. Van der Kolk, Alexander C. McFarlane, and Lars Weisaeth, eds. *Traumatic Stress: The Effects of Overwhelming Experience on Mind, Body, and Society.,* (New York: The Guilford Press, 1996), 3–5

42. Richard Pierce, "Re: Update," Email messaage to the author, March 30, 2006.

43. Tick, *War and the Soul,* 99.

44. Van der Kolk, McFarlane, and Weisaeth, *Traumatic Stress,* 6.

45. Mike Lewis, "Vietnam, Iraq wars cited for minister's suicide," *Seattle Post-Intelligencer,* February 22, 2005, http://seattlepi.nwsource.com/local/213046_priestsuicide22.html.

3. MARCH

1. Joe Dennis, "Our Flag is Flying With Pride and a Lot of Apprehension," *Grant County Journal,* September 12, 2001.

2. "List of Casualties," *San Diego Union-Tribune,* March 31, 2004, http://www.signonsandiego.com/news/world/iraq/memorial/sidebarresult.php?month=March&year=2004.

3. Ibid.

4. Ibid.

5. Erin Emery and Eileen Kelley, "Ft. Carson Green Beret's death raises questions about help for GI stress," *Denver Post,* March 17, 2004.

6. Jim Spencer, "Iraq veteran's death serves as a warning," *Denver Post,* March 21, 2004.

7. Jeffrey Gettleman, "Soldier Accused as Coward Says He Is Guilty Only of Panic Attack," *New York Times,* November 6, 2003.

8. "Stressed-out Soldiers," *CBS Evening News,* July 12, 2006, http://www.cbsnews.com/stories/2006/07/12/eveningnews/main1798343.shtml; Michael de Yoanna, "Patterns of Misconduct," *Colorado Springs Independent,* July 13–19, 2006, http://www.csindy.com/csindy/2006-07-13/cover.html; Daniel Zwerdling, "Soldiers Say Army Ignores, Punishes Mental Anguish," *All Things Considered,* NPR, December 4, 2006, http://www.npr.org/templates/story/story.php?storyId=6576505.

9. Mark Benjamin and Dan Olmsted, "Exclusive: Green Beret's strange suicide," *United Press International,* May 14, 2004.

10. Mark Benjamin, "Seventh Iraq war veteran kills himself," *United Press International,* March 17, 2004.

11. Jim Spencer, "GI's suicide shows failure by all of us," *The Denver Post,* March 21, 2004.

12. M.L. Lyke, "The War Comes Home: Rifleman couldn't take any more," *Seattle Post-Intelligencer*, August 13, 2004, http://seattlepi.nwsource.com/local/186127_warsuicide13.html.

13. *Army Medical Department, News and Media*, "Army Medical Evacuation Statistics for OIF & OEF," August 19, 2004, http://www.armymedicine.army.mil/default2.htm.

14. Eric Schmitt, "U.S. Army Finds Its Suicide Rate in Iraq is Higher Than for Other G.I.'s," *New York Times*, March 26, 2004.

15. Lynda Hurst, "Troops in Iraq on Suicide Watch," *Toronto Star*, April 11, 2004.

16. United States General Accounting Office, "Defense Health Care: Quality Assurance Process Needed to Improve Force Health Protection and Surveillance," *Report to the Chairman and Ranking Minority Member, Subcommittee on Total Force, Committee on Armed Services, House of Representatives*, September 2003, http://www.gao.gov/new.items/d031041.pdf.

17. Bryan Bender, "Officials gathering data, but advocates push for more," *Boston Globe*, March 20, 2004, http://www.boston.com/news/nation/articles/2004/03/20/officials_gathering_data_but_advocates_push_for_more/.

18. David Goldstein, "Some Guard, Reserve sent to Iraq with doubtful health," *Kansas City Star*, March 25, 2004.

19. Bruce Alpert, "Veterans Protest Reduced Medical Exams for Returning Soldiers," *Newhouse News Service*, March 20, 2004, http://www.newhousenews.com/archive/alpert031904.html.

20. Laura Kent, "Re: OEF/OIF PTSD Book - Phillip Kent piece for your review," Email message to author, August 26, 2006.

21. Dave Conger, "Shockwave," *The Carolina Reporter*, September 12, 2001, http://www.dailygamecock.com/media/storage/paper247/news/2001/09/12/News/Shockwave-92510.shtml?norewrite200608130555&sourcedomain=www.dailygamecock.com.

22. "Soldiers of the Gauntlet," *720ᵗʰ Military Police Battalion Newsletter*, November 2003, 1, http://www.720mp.org/november03.pdf.

23. Jess Bravin, "Army Report Omitted Prison Details," *Wall Street Journal*, June 4, 2004.

24. Steven H. Miles, M.D., "Medical Investigations of Homicides of Prisoners of War in Iraq and Afghanistan," *Newsletter on Philosophy and Medicine* 5, no. 1 (2005), http://www.apa.udel.edu/apa/publications/newsletters/MedicineNL/v05n1.htm.

25. Yossef Bodansky, *The Secret History of the Iraq War*, (New York: Regan Books, 2004), 468–473.

26. Wade Hampton, "Info on Lt. Phillip Kent/suicide from his mother," Email message to the author, June 29, 2006.

PART II—A GLIMPSE IN THE MIRROR

1. Van der Kolk, McFarlane, and Weisaeth, *Traumatic Stress,* 408.

4. MEDIA, SOCIETY AND THE PACKAGING OF WAR

1. Chris Hedges, *War Is a Force That Gives Us Meaning* (New York: Anchor Books, 2003), 5.

2. Bill McKibben, *The Age of Missing Information* (New York: Plume, 1992), 9.

3. *Pew Research Center,* "News Audiences Increasingly Politicized," June 8, 2004, http://people-press.org/reports/display.php3?PageID=833.

4. Martin Merzer, "Americans are against unilateral war in Iraq," *Knight Ridder News Service,* January 15, 2003.

5. Merzer, "Americans are against unilateral war in Iraq."

6. Dana Milbank and Claudia Deane, "Hussein Link to 9/11 Lingers in Many Minds," *Washington Post,* September 6, 2003, http://www.washingtonpost.com/ac2/wp-dyn?pagename=article&contentId=A32862-2003Sep5.

7. *Zogby International,* "Zogby Poll: 9/11 + 5 Reveals Dramatic Partisan Split," September 5, 2006, http://www.zogby.com/News/ReadNews.dbm?ID=1169.

8. The belief that Saddam Hussein was responsible in some way for the attacks of September 11, 2001 continues to hold (though waning) with some Americans, even though those charges have been discredited. In February 2005, 64% believed Saddam Hussein had "strong links" to al Qaeda; by December, the number had fallen to 41%. "Sizeable Minorities Still Believe Saddam Hussein Had Strong Links to Al Qaeda, Helped Plan 9/11 and Had Weapons of Mass Destruction," *PR Newswire,* December 29, 2005, http://www.prnewswire.com/cgi-bin/stories.pl?ACCT=104&STORY=/www/story/12-29-2005/0004240417&EDATE=.

9. When pressed, President Bush has repeatedly confirmed that there was no connection whatsoever between Saddam Hussein and the September 11, 2001 attacks. September 17, 2003—"No, we've had no evidence that Saddam Hussein was involved with September the 11th." March 20, 2006—"First, just if I might correct a misperception, I don't think we ever said—at least I know I didn't say that there was a direct connection between September the 11th and Saddam Hussein." August 21, 2006, answering the question 'What did Iraq have to do with...the attack on the World Trade Center?'—"Nothing. Except it's part of—and nobody has suggested in this administration that Saddam Hussein ordered the attack. Iraq was a—Iraq—the lesson of September 11th is take threats before they fully materialize, Ken. Nobody's ever suggested that the attacks of September the 11th were ordered by Iraq." All quotes available at ThinkProgress.org.

10. Julia Baird, "Just a change of masters for Iraq press," Sydney *Morning*

Herald, December 8, 2005, http://www.smh.com.au/news/opinion/just-a-change-of-masters-for-iraq-press/2005/12/07/1133829660308.html.

11. Seemingly giving strength to the study results, very few American media outlets reported on the MTSU study even though the information might have been considered newsworthy to the American public. "Poll: Americans Concerned About Media Truth-Telling, Excess," *Newswise,* December 12, 2006, http://www.newswise.com/articles/view/525846/; Colleen Creamer, "Poll respondents criticize media for bias, deception," *Murfreesboro Daily News Journal,* December 12, 2006, http://dnj.midsouthnews.com/apps/pbcs.dll/article?AID=/20061212/NEWS01/612120329/1002.

12. Dan Farber, "Dan Rather on the state of American media," *ZDNet,* April 26, 2006, http://blogs.zdnet.com/BTL/?p=2927.

13. Mark Emmert, "Keep Ideas Flowing Freely," *Seattle Times,* December 22, 2006.

14. Eric Alterman, *What Liberal Media? The Truth About Bias and the News* (New York: Basic Books, 2003), 216.

15. From The Editors, "The Times and Iraq," *The New York Times,* May 26, 2004.

16. Howard Kurtz, "The Post on WMDs: An Inside Story," *Washington Post,* August 12, 2004, http://www.washingtonpost.com/ac2/wp-dyn/A58127-2004Aug11?language=printer.

17. Howard Kurtz, "New Republic Editors 'Regret' Their Support of Iraq War," *Washington Post,* June 19, 2004, http://www.washingtonpost.com/wp-dyn/articles/A53812-2004Jun18.html.

18. "Washington Post Admits It Buried Anti-War Voices Before the Iraq invasion," *Democracy Now!,* August 13, 2004, http://www.democracynow.org/article.pl?sid=04/08/13/1413248.

19. Bill Carter, "MSNBC Cancels Phil Donahue," *New York Times,* February 26, 2003, http://www.nytimes.com/2003/02/26/business/media/26PHIL.html?ex=1156824000&en=b2531eab97d43997&ei=5070.

20. *FAIR: Fairness & Accuracy in Reporting,* Press release, "Some Critical Media Voices Face Censorship," April 3, 2003, http://www.fair.org/index.php?page=1825.

21. "Names of U.S. war dead read on 'Nightline,'" *Associated Press,* May 1, 2004.

22. "'Nightline' Controversy," *CNN Live From...,* April 30, 2004, http://transcripts.cnn.com/TRANSCRIPTS/0404/30/lol.01.html

23. "McCain rebukes Sinclair 'Nightline' decision," *CNN,* April 20, 2004, http://www.cnn.com/2004/SHOWBIZ/TV/04/29/abc.nightline/index.html

24. George W. Bush, "President Launches "Lessons of Liberty," (October 30,

2001), http://www.whitehouse.gov/news/releases/ 2001/10/20011030-7.html.

25. Jacqui Goddard, "US Idol More Popular Than The pPresident," *The Scotsman*, May 26, 2006, http://news.scotsman.com/international.cfm?id=778702006.

26. Hedges, *War is a Force That Give Us Meaning*, 26.

27. Van der Kolk, McFarlane, and Weisaeth, *Traumatic Stress* 27.

28. John Crawford, *The Last True Story I'll Ever Tell: An Accidental Soldier's Account of the War in Iraq*, (New York: Riverhead Books, 2005), xiii.

5. LEADERSHIP, POLITICS AND THE PRICE OF WAR

1. Richard B. Cheney, "Vice President's Remarks at a Rally for the Troops at Offutt Air Force Base," (August 29, 2006), http://www.whitehouse.gov/news/releases/2006/08/20060829-4.html.

2. George W. Bush, "President's Address to the Nation," (September 11, 2006), http://www.whitehouse.gov/news/releases/2006/09/20060911-3.html.

3. Thomas L. Friedman, "The Home Team," *New York Times*, February 8, 2004.

4. Tom Brokaw, *The Greatest Generation* (New York: Random House, 1998), inside cover.

5. Jenna Ross, "'Why We Fight' director pulls no punches," *The Minnesota Daily*, February 23, 2006, http://www.mndaily.com/articles/2006/02/22/67271.

6. Richard Benedetto and Susan Page, "Bush's job approval lowest since 9/11," *USA Today*, January 13, 2003, http://www.usatoday.com/news/politicselections/2003-01-13-bush-poll_x.htm.

7. The sole dissenting voice, Rep. Barbara Lee [D-CA], explained her decision, saying, "I am convinced that military action will not prevent further acts of international terrorism against the United States. Finally, we must be careful not to embark on an open-ended war with neither an exit strategy nor a focused target." In a later interview, she referred to her training as a social worker saying, "Right now, we're dealing with recovery, and we're dealing with mourning, and there's no way... [we should]... deal with decisions that could escalate violence and spiral out of control." "Congress approves resolution authorizing force," *CNN*, September 15, 2001, http://archives.cnn.com/2001/US/09/14/congress.terrorism; "Congresswoman Barbara Lee Explains Her Lone Vote," *Hip Hop and Politics*, September 18, 2001, http://www.daveyd.com/barbaraleevotepolitics.html.

8. George W. Bush, "Address to a Joint Session of Congress and the American People," (September 20, 2001), http://www.whitehouse.gov/news/releases/2001/09/20010920-8.html.

9. Ibid.

10. "President Bush talks to Brian Williams," *NBC Nightly News*, August 29, 2006, http://msnbc.msn.com/id/14576012.

11. Sean D. Naylor, "7th Cavalry inflicts heavy casualties in running battle," *USA Today*, March 25, 2003, http://www.usatoday.com/news/world/iraq/2003-03-25-war-zone_x.htm.

12. Christian Lowe, "Photographer finds boy from famous picture," *USA Today*, July 7, 2003, http://www.usatoday.com/news/world/iraq/2003-07-06-photo-boy_x.htm.

13. "Image of soldier, boy explains mission," *USA Today*, March 31, 2003.

14. Much of the detail in this section from Indrani Sen, "From war hero to war haunted," *New York Newsday*, October 23, 2005, http://www.newsday.com/news/nationworld/world/ny-liptsd2344815260ct23,0,5713254.story.

15. Naylor, "7th Cavalry inflicts heavy casualties in running battle."

16. Daniel Borunda, "Medic in rescue photo arrested," *El Paso Times*, October 29, 2006.

17. N.J. Burkett, "One Long Island Soldier Was Called A Hero When He Rescued An Iraqi Child," *WABC-TV*, October 10, 2005, http://abclocal.go.com/wabc/story?section=local&id=3523434.

18. George W. Bush, "President Bush Delivers State of the Union Address," (January 31, 2006), http://www.whitehouse.gov/news/releases/2006/01/20060131-10.html.

19. U.S. Senate Committee on Veterans' Affairs, Press Release, "Craig Reacts to Historic Budget Increase for Veterans—$80.6 Billion for 2007," (February 6, 2006), http://veterans.senate.gov/index.cfm?FuseAction=Newsroom.PressReleases&id=445.

20. Kelley Beaucar Vlahos, "Vets' Mental Health Needs Intensify," *FOX News*, April 3, 2006, http://www.foxnews.com/story/0,2933,190396,00.html; Andrew Taylor, "Bush plan cuts vets' care in '08," *Seattle Post-Intelligencer*, February 28, 2006.

21. House Committee on Veterans' Affairs – Democratic Office, News Release, "GAO Audit Indicates VA Budget Sham," (February 2, 2006), http://veterans.house.gov/democratic/press/109th/2-2-06gao.htm.

22. U.S. Government Accountability Office, *Veteran Affairs: Limited Support for Reported Health Care Management Efficiency Savings*, (February 1, 2006), http://www.gao.gov/new.items/d06359r.pdf.

23. House Committee on Veterans' Affairs – Democratic Office, "GAO Audit Indicates VA Budget Sham."

24. David Axe, "Vets Struggle With Life After War," *Military.com*, May 24, 2006, http://www.military.com/NewsContent/0,13319,98362,00.html.

25. "GAO Report Amplifies the Need for Assured Funding of VA Health Care," *U.S.Newswire*, February 2, 2006, http://releases.usnewswire.com/GetRelease.asp?id=60498

26. The following list written by the Democratic staff of the House Veterans' Affairs Committee, "Snapshot of How VA Budget Shortfall is Hurting Veterans'

Access to Safe and Timely Care across the Nation," (June 29, 2005), http://veterans. house.gov/democratic/budget/snapshot6-29-05.htm.

28. "PTSD Care Demand Taxing System," *Bangor Daily News*, June 21, 2006, http://www.military.com/NewsContent/0,13319,102159,00.html

28. U.S. Government Accountability Office, "VA Health Care: Preliminary Findings on the Dept. of Veterans Affairs Health Care Budget Formulation for Fiscal Years 2005 and 2006," (February 6, 2006), http://www.gao.gov/new.items/d06430r.pdf

29. Shankar Vedantam, "A Political Debate On Stress Disorder," *Washington Post*, December 27, 2005, http://www.washingtonpost.com/wp-dyn/content/article/2005/12/26/AR2005122600792.html.

30. Ryan Holeywell, "Critics blast veterans' mental health care," *United Press International*, July 30, 2005.

31. Donna St. George, "Female Iraq vet is home but still haunted," *Washington Post*, August 20, 2006, http://www.msnbc.msn.com/id/14431097.

32. The Hines VA Hospital (Illinois) now routinely screens every veteran it sees for PTSD.

33. Pat Cunningham, "Kingston GI brought home hidden injuries," *Rockford Register Star*, April 16, 2006.

34. Cindy Stauffer, "The War Within: Some Iraq Vets Coming Home with Emotional Scars That Are Difficult to Heal," *Lancaster New Era*, April 21, 2006.

35. Rick Rogers, "Vets' mental health focus of conference," *San Diego Union-Tribune*, April 29, 2006, http://www.signonsandiego.com/uniontrib/20060429/news_7m29mental.html.

36. Scott, Wilbur J., *Vietnam Veterans Since the War: The Politics of Ptsd, Agent Orange, and the National Memorial* (University of Oklahoma Press, 2004), 27–28.

37. "Three Lives Brightened by 'Deadly Nightshade,'" *Life*, September 17, 1945, 138.

38. Shephard, *A War of Nerves*, 355.

39. Dennis Conrad, "Brecksville VA hospital takes lead in treatment of Viet vets' trauma," *Associated Press*, December 8, 1985.

40. Vedantam, "A Political Debate On Stress Disorder."

41. Cory Reiss, "VA predicts cost of disability pay for vets will soar," *The Gainesville Sun*, December 3, 2006, http://www.gainesville.com/apps/pbcs.dll/article?AID=/20061203/WIRE/612020333/-1/news.

42. Democratic Policy Committee, "Monthly National Security Index," (July 20, 2006), http://democrats.senate.gov/dpc/dpc-new.cfm?doc_name=fs-109-2-112.

43. Rebecca Carroll, "VA to review veterans' PTSD cases," *Associated Press*, August 12, 2005.

44. Mark Benjamin, "The V.A.'s bad review," *Salon*, October 26, 2005, http://dir.salon.com/story/news/feature/2005/10/26/suicide/index.html.

45. Institute of Medicine of the National Academies, Board on Population Health and Public Health Practice, Committee on Gulf War and Health, *Posttraumatic Stress Disorder: Diagnosis and Assessment*, (Washington, DC: National Academies Press, 2006).

46. Aaron Levin, "VA to Keep Using DSM To Diagnose PTSD in Vets," *Psychiatric News* 41, no. 14 (July 21, 2006), 1, http://pn.psychiatryonline.org/cgi/content/full/41/14/1.

47. "War Veterans Feeling Stressed, Deserted," *CBS News*, July 12, 2006, http://cbs11tv.com/topstories/topstories_story_193204627.html.

48. D.E. Ford, M.S.W., Commander Jeff Huber, I.L. Meagher, "Blaming the Veteran: The Politics of Post Traumatic Stress Disorder," *ePluribus Media*, February 11, 2006, http://www.epluribusmedia.org/features/20060206PTSD_intro.html.

49. Jeff Huber, "Re: PSTD—updates of where we are," Email message to author, January 31, 2006.

50. Gregg Zotoya, "Troubled troops in no-win plight," *USA Today*, November 2, 2006, http://www.usatoday.com/news/nation/2006-11-01-troubled-troops_x.htm.

51. Quotes and detail in the Doherty story from Thomas Doherty, "Iraq, PTSD, marijuana use and Other-than-honorable discharged," Email message to author, June 29, 2006.

52. "101st Airborne Division Soldier Receives Silver Star," *American Forces Press Service*, February 11, 2004, http://www.defendamerica.mil/profiles/feb2004/pr021204a.html.

53. Kimberly Hefling, "War hero faces setbacks after returning home from Iraq," *Associated Press*, March 24, 2004.

54. DoD spending figures as of February 2006: Iraq, $4.5 billion per month; Afghanistan, $800 million per month. Mark Mazzetti and Joel Havemann, "Bush's Bill for War Is Rising," *Los Angeles Times*, February 3, 2006.

55. Stephen L. Robinson, "Hidden Toll of the War in Iraq: Mental Health and the Military," *National Gulf War Resource Center* and *Center for American Progress*, September 2004, http://www.americanprogress.org/kf/hiddentoll91404.pdf .

56. Linda Bilmes and Joseph E. Stiglitz, "The Economic Costs of the Iraq War: An Appraisal Three Years After the Beginning of the Conflict," Paper prepared for presentation at ASSA meetings, Boston January 2006, http://www2.gsb.columbia.edu/faculty/jstiglitz/Cost_of_War_in_Iraq.pdf.

6. THE RUMSFELD REVOLUTION IN MILITARY AFFAIRS

1. Governor George W. Bush, "A Period of Consequences," The Citadel, September 23, 1999.

2. Ibid.

3. Michael R. Gordon and David S. Cloud, "Rumsfeld Memo Proposed 'Major Adjustment' in Iraq," *New York Times*, December 3, 2006.

4. Ibid.

5. Thomas E. Ricks, *Fiasco: The American Military Adventure in Iraq*, (New York: The Penguin Press, 2006), 169.

6. Andrew J. Bacevich, *The New American Militarism: How Americans Are Seduced by War*, (New York: Oxford University Press, 2005), 147.

7. Harold Kennedy, "Army Undergoing Biggest Makeover Since World War II," *National Defense Magazine*, October 2004, http://www.nationaldefensemagazine. org/issues/2004/oct/Army_Undergoing.htm.

8. Bacevich, *The New American Militarism*, 64.

9. Ibid., 167.

10. Ibid.,168.

11. William R. Hawkins, "Is Rumsfeld's 'Revolution in Military Affairs' Finally Over?" *American Economic Alert*, September 12, 2006, http://www. americaneconomicalert.org/view_art.asp?Prod_ID=2548.

12. Ricks, *Fiasco*, 411.

13. James Kitfield, "Rumsfeld leaves his successor in a difficult position," *National Journal*, December 18, 2006, http://www.govexec.com/dailyfed/1206/ 121806nj1.htm.

14. Jonathan Shay, "Ethics, Leadership, Policy - Not Separate Spheres," (lecture, Naval Postgraduate School, Monterey, California, May 19, 1998), http://www. belisarius.com/modern_business_strategy/shay/shay_prevent_psy_injury.htm.

15. Kitfield, "Rumsfeld Leaves His Successor In A Difficult Position."

16. U.S. Senate Democratic Policy Committee, *An Oversight Hearing on the Planning and Conduct of the War in Iraq: Colonel Thomas X. Hammes*, September 25, 2006, http://democrats.senate.gov/dpc/hearings/hearing38/hammes.pdf,

17. "4th Infantry Division (Mechanized) "Ivy Division"/ "Iron Horse"," *GlobalSecurity. org*, undated, http://www.globalsecurity.org/military/agency/army/4id.htm.

18. Perry Jefferies, "Providing for the Troops," *Iraq and Afghanistan Veterans of America*, undated, http://www.optruth.org/index.php?option=content&task=view &id=99&Itemid=119.

19. Ray Suarez, "Under Armored," *PBS Newshour with Jim Lehrer*, December 9, 2004, http://www.pbs.org/newshour/bb/military/july-dec04/armor_12-9.html#.

20. "Forces: U.S. & Coalition/Army," *CNN International*, undated, http:// edition.cnn.com/SPECIALS/2003/iraq/forces/coalition/deployment/army/2nd. armored.cavalry.html; Sandra Jontz, "Scribblings on walls tell tales of 'one-way prison' in Iraq," *Stars and Stripes*, June 10, 2003, http://www.estripes.com/article.asp ?section=104&article=15350&archive=true; Warren Richey, "In gun seizures, some

surprise finds," *Christian Science Monitor*, May 15, 2003, http://www.csmonitor. com/2003/0515/p02s01-woiq.html; Jason Kennickell, "2nd ACR raid in Iraq successful due to training," *Second Cavalry Association, Inc.*, November 22, 2003.

21. Ricks, *Fiasco*, 216.

22. "November—2003 Image of the Month," *U.S. Army IV*, November 2003, http://www4.army.mil/doim/iotm_all.php?ImageID=37; Ricks, *Fiasco*, 247–249.

23. Capt. Sean P. Kirley, "SECDEF meets 2nd ACR Dragoons, views ICDC," *1st Armored Division: The Old Ironsides Report*, February 25, 2004, http://www.arcent. army.mil/news_letters/2004/february/25feb%20old%20ironsides%20report.pdf#s earch=%22ICDC%202nd%20ACR%22

24. Sgt. Susan German, "Classwork Complete, Iraqi NCOs Ready to Lead," *Defend America: U.S. Department of Defense News About the War On Terrorism*, March 11, 2004, http://www.defendamerica.mil/articles/mar2004/a031504j.html.

25. DarkSyde, "Interview With a Combat Vet," *Daily Kos*, September 14, 2006, http://www.dailykos.com/story/2006/9/14/74637/0622.

26. Rowan Scarborough, "Army unit claims victory over sheik," *Washington Times*, June 23, 2004, http://www.washingtontimes.com/national/20040622-113720-3352r. htm.

27. "Thousands of U.S. Troops Getting Ready to Go Home; Dick Cheney Campaigns in Middle America," *CNN Sunday Morning*, July 4, 2004, http:// transcripts.cnn.com/TRANSCRIPTS/0407/04/sm.02.html.

28. "2nd Cavalry Regiment," *GlobalSecurity.org*, undated, http://www.global security.org/military/agency/army/2acr.htm.

29. U.S. Army, *Combat Action Badge*, http://www.army.mil/symbols/combat badges/Action.html?story_id_key=7285.

30. "Tacoma police say soldier died of gunshot at home," *Tacoma News Tribune*, August 6, 2005.

31. "Army Specialist Laid to Rest," *KQTV*, August 3, 2005, http://www.kq2. com/news/default.asp?mode=shownews&id=2201.

7. 21ST CENTURY WARFARE AND PTSD

1. Theodore Nadelson, MA, MD. *Trained to Kill: Soldiers at War*, (Baltimore: John Hopkins University Press, 2005), 37.

2. Zack Bazzi, Interview with author, June 19, 2006, http://www.ptsdcombat. com/audio/war-tapes_bazzi-interview.mp3

3. Jeff Tietz, "The Killing Factory," *Rolling Stone*, April 20, 2006, 54.

4. Dave Grossman, *On Killing: The Psychological Cost of Learning to Kill in War and Society*, (New York: Back Bay Books, 1995), 4.

5. Hedges, *What Every Person Should Know About War*, 75.

6. Zucchino, "Iconic Marine is Home but Not at Ease."

7. Tietz, "The Killing Factory," 57.

8. Kara Platoni, "The Pentagon Goes to the Video Arcade—video games used as military training," *The Progressive*, July 1999.

9. Tietz, "The Killing Factory," 58.

10. Peter Kilner, "Military Leaders' Obligation to Justify Killing in War," *Military Review*, March/April 2002, 25.

11. Dan Baum, "The Price of Valor," *The New Yorker*, July 12 and 19, 2004, http://www.newyorker.com/fact/content/articles/040712fa_fact.

12. Kilner, "Military Leaders' Obligation to Justify Killing in War," 28.

13. Baum, "The Price of Valor."

14. Kilner, "Military Leaders' Obligation to Justify Killing in War," 30–31.

15. Baum, "The Price of Valor."

16. Kilner, "Military Leaders' Obligation to Justify Killing in War."

17. Baum, "The Price of Valor."

18. Yvonne Latty, *In Conflict: Iraq War Veterans Speak Out on Duty, Loss, and the Fight to Stay Alive*, (Sausalito: PoliPointPress, 2006), 132

19. *Zogby International*, "U.S. Troops in Iraq: 72% Say End War in 2006," February 28, 2006, http://www.zogby.com/news/ReadNews.dbm?ID=1075.

20. Bryan Bender, "Concern voiced on multiple tours of duty," *Boston Globe*, November 11, 2005, http://www.boston.com/news/world/articles/2005/11/11/concern_voiced_on_multiple_tours_of_duty.

21. Rick Rogers, "Some troops headed back to Iraq are mentally ill," *San Diego Union-Tribune*, March 19, 2006, http://www.signonsandiego.com/news/military/20060319-9999-1n19mental.html.

22. Leo Shane III, "Boxer: DOD slow to implement new mental health task force," *Stars and Stripes*, May 4, 2006, http://www.estripes.com/article.asp?section=104&article=36054&archive=true.

23. U.S. Government Accountability Office, "Post Traumatic Stress Disorder: DOD Needs to Identify the Factors Its Providers Use to Make Mental Health Evaluation Referrals to Servicemembers," *report to Congressional Committees*, May 2006, http://www.gao.gov/new.items/d06397.pdf.

24. Lisa Chedekel and Matthew Kauffman, "Mentally Unfit, Forced To Fight," *Hartford Courant*, May 14, 2006, http://www.courant.com/hc-mental1a.artmay14,0,275720.story?coll=hc-headlines-home.

25. Rogers, "Some troops headed back to Iraq are mentally ill."

26. Mark Clinton and Tony Udell, "The Suicide of an Iraq War Veteran," *Counterpunch.org*, October 5, 2004, http://www.counterpunch.org/clinton10052004.html.

27. M. L. Lyke, "The unseen cost of war: American minds," *Seattle Post-Intelligencer*, August 27, 2004, http://seattlepi.nwsource.com/local/188143_ptsd27.html.

28. Dave Grossman, *On Combat: The Psychology and Physiology of Deadly Conflict in War and in Peace*, (Belleville: PPCT Research Publications, 2004), 12, 21-27.

29. Gabriel, *No More Heroes*, 119-124.

30. Eric Massa, "The Iraq War PTSD Epidemic," *Securing America Community*, May 14, 2006, http://securingamerica.com/ccn/node/6054.

31. Peter Beaumont, "Stress epidemic strikes American forces in Iraq," *The Observer*, January 24, 2004, http://observer.guardian.co.uk/international/story/0,6903,1130771,00.html.

32. Cahal Milmo, "Suicide Soldier's Dying Words to His Mother: 'I can't go to Iraq. I can't kill those children'," *The Independent*, August 25, 2006.

33. Pamela Martineau and Steve Wiegand, "Women at War," *Sacramento Bee*, March 6, 2005, http://www.sacbee.com/content/news/projects/women_at_war/story/12519110p-13374582c.html.

34. Sharon Cohen, "Women in War: Iraq and Afghanistan," *Associated Press*, December 4, 2006.

35. Rowan Scarborough and Joseph Curl, "Despite pressure, Bush vows 'no women in combat'," *Washington Times*, January 12, 2005, http://www.washtimes.com/national/20050111-101005-5277r.htm.

36. Martineau and Wiegand, "Women at War."

37. Joseph Shapiro, "A Woman Guard Member's Struggle with PTSD," *NPR Morning Edition*, June 2, 2005, http://www.npr.org/templates/story/story.php?storyId=4676372.

38. Martha Brant, "'I Was Shell Shocked'," *Newsweek*, July 5, 2005, http://www.msnbc.msn.com/id/8471505/site/newsweek/.

39. Jason Johns, "Is The War In Iraq Worth It?," *Wisconsin State Journal*, November 27, 2005, http://www.madison.com/archives/read.php?ref=/wsj/2005/11/27/0511260172.php.

40. Brant, "'I Was Shell Shocked'."

41. Abbie Pickett, personal interview with author, June 9, 2006.

42. Wayne Woolley, "Marines know after 48 hours, 'It is time to rock'," *New Jersey Star-Ledger*, March 19, 2003, http://www.nj.com/war/ledger/index.ssf?/news/stories/0319iraq.html.

43. Crawford, *The Last True Story I'll Ever Tell*, xii.

44. "Help Wanted," Editorial, *Hampton Roads Daily Press*, August 7, 2006; Stephen M. Duncan, "A 'War of a Different Kind' and the Reconstruction of the U.S. Reserve Forces," *Foreign Policy Research Institute*, December 6, 2004, http://www.fpri.org/transcripts/lecture.20041206.duncan.wardifferentkindreserves.html

45. Stephen Spotswood, "Returnees With PTSD At Risk Of Suicide In Cases,"

U.S. Medicine, September 2005, http://www.usmedicine.com/article.cfm?articleID =1154&issueID=79.

46. Charles Moskos, "Toward a New Conception of the Citizen Soldier," *Foreign Policy Research Institute*, April 7, 2005, http://www.fpri.org/enotes/20050407. military.moskos.newconceptioncitizensoldier.html.

47. Ann Scott Tyson, "Army Using Policy to Deny Reserve Officer Resignations," *Washington Post*, May 11, 2006, http://www.washingtonpost.com/wp-dyn/content/article/2006/05/10/AR2006051002061.html.

48. John Riley, "Battle-tested soldier defeated back at home," *Chicago Tribune*, April 22, 2004.

49. "Reservist Commits Suicide After Return," *Associated Press*, March 19, 2004.

8. IDEALISM, GUILT AND THE DEGENERATION OF WAR

1. "Marines Killed In Tanker Plane Crash," *Arlington National Cemetery Website*, January 9, 2002, http://www.arlingtoncemetery.net/010902-crash.htm.

2. Sarah Farmer, "IN MEMORIAM: Sgt. Jeffrey Michael Lehner," *The Independent*, January 12, 2006.

3. Ann Louise Bardach, "For one Marine, torture came home," *Los Angeles Times*, February 14, 2006.

4. Bardach, "For one Marine, torture came home."

5. Jeff Davis as told to staff writer David Perlmutt, "'All my life, we were the good guys.'," *Charlotte Observer*, Opinion, September 10, 2006, http://www.charlotte.com/mld/charlotte/news/special_packages/sept11/15483868.htm.

6. Edward Fadeley and Joyce Gall, "Terrorism bill ignores basic U.S. principles," *Oregon Register-Guard*, Opinion, September 29, 2006, http://www.registerguard.com/news/2006/09/29/ed.col.fadeley.0929.p1.php?section=opinion.

7. Hamdan v. Rumsfeld (No. 05-184) 415 F. 3d 33," *Cornell Law School:Supreme Court Collection*, http://www.law.cornell.edu/supct/html/05-184.ZS.html.;"Rubber stamping violations in the "war on terror": Congress fails human rights," *Amnesty International*, September 29, 2006, http://www.amnestyusa.org/news/document.do?id=ENGAMR511552006.

8. Karen DeYoung and Peter Baker, "Bush Detainee Plan Adds to World Doubts Of U.S., Powell Says," *Washington Post*, September 19, 2006, http://www.washingtonpost.com/wp-dyn/content/article/2006/09/18/AR2006091801414.html.

9. Grossman, *On Killing*, 205.

10. Moskos, "Toward a New Conception of the Citizen Soldier.

11. T. Christian Miller, "Soldier's journey ends in anguish," *Los Angeles Times*, December 4, 2005.

12. William M. Arkin, "Rumsfeld's Enemy: It's Us," *Washington Post*, August 30, 2006,http://blog.washingtonpost.com/earlywarning/2006/08/rumsfelds_declaration_of_war_o.html#more.

13. Eli Sanders, "Putting the Iraq War on Trial," *Time*, August 18, 2006, http://www.time.com/time/nation/article/0,8599,1228779,00.html.

14. Hal Bernton, "Officer at Fort Lewis calls Iraq war illegal, refuses order to go," *Seattle Times*, June 7, 2006, http://seattletimes.nwsource.com/html/localnews/2003044627_nogo7m.html.

15. Mike Barber, "Hearing for soldier who won't serve in Iraq puts war on trial," *Seattle Post-Intelligencer*, August 18, 2006.

16. Gregg Kakesako, "New Trial Date Set for Watada," *Honolulu Star-Bulletin*, February 28, 2007.

17. Nicosia, *Home to War*, 158–59.

18. Tick, *War and Soul*, 160.

19. Rone Tempest, "Bloody Scenes Haunt a Marine; Member of a unit under investigation recalls a day in Iraq that claimed a buddy and civilians," *Los Angeles Times*, May 29, 2006.

20. Ellen Kickmeyer, "In Haditha, Memories of a Massacre," *Washington Post*, May 27, 2006, http://www.washingtonpost.com/wp-dyn/content/article/2006/05/26/AR2006052602069.html.

21. Tempest, "Bloody Scenes Haunt a Marine."

22. Paul von Zielbauer and Carolyn Marshall, "Marines Charge 4 With Murder of Iraq Civilians," *New York Times*, December 22, 2006.

23. Jonathan Shay, MD, PhD, *Achilles in Vietnam: Combat Trauma and the Undoing of Character*, (New York: Scribner, 1994), 80.

24. Ricks, *Fiasco*, 272.

25. Shephard, *A War of Nerves*, 372.

26. Hedges, *War Is a Force That Gives Us Meaning*, 86.

27. "Marines 'Traumatized' By Iraqi Deaths," *CBS/Associated Press*, May 30, 2006, http://www.cbsnews.com/stories/2006/05/30/iraq/main1665030.shtml.

28. Tempest, "Bloody Scenes Haunt a Marine;" Pablo Lopez, "Iraq vet charged in Hanford wreck," *The Fresno Bee*, June 3, 2006.

29. Irene Sege, "Something happened to Jeff," *Boston Globe*, March 1, 2005, http://www.boston.com/yourlife/health/mental/articles/2005/03/01/jeff_lucey_returned_from_iraq_a_changed_man_then_he_killed_himself?pg=full.

30. George W. Bush, "President Says Saddam Hussein Must Leave Iraq Within 48 Hours," March 17, 2003, http://www.whitehouse.gov/news/releases/2003/03/20030317-7.html.

31. Kevin and Joyce Lucey, *OEF/OIF Written History Survey Form*, received by the author on August 11, 2006.

32. Mehul Srivastava, "Swallowed by Pain," *Dayton Daily News*, October 11, 2004, http://www.daytondailynews.com/project/content/project/suicide/daily/1011lucey.html.

33. Commanders and Staff of the 1st FSSG, "Brute Force Combat Service Support: 1st Force Service Support Group in Operation IRAQI FREEDOM," *Marine Corps Gazette*, August 2003, 34–38.

34. Christopher Buchanan, "A Reporter's Journey," *Frontline*, March 1, 2005, http://www.pbs.org/wgbh/pages/frontline/shows/heart/lucey.

35. Lucey, *OEF/OIF Written History Survey Form*.

36. Newt, "The Things He Carried: Atrocities, Investigations and the Suicide of Lance Corporal Jeffrey Lucey," *This is Rumor Control*, August 20, 2004, http://www.thisisrumorcontrol.org/node/370\\\\\\\.

37. "Parents Mourn Son's Suicide After Returning From Iraq Duty: "He's a Casualty of War But He'll Never Be Known As That"," *Democracy Now*, August 11, 2004, http://democracynow.org/article.pl?sid=04/08/11/145205.

38. Sege, "Something happened to Jeff."

PART III—A CALL TO ARMS

1. Byron Pitts, "From Hero To Homeless," *CBS*, Evening News March 25, 2005, http://www.cbsnews.com/stories/2005/03/25/eveningnews/main683247.shtml.

9. RETURNING TO A FOREIGN WORLD

1. Penny Coleman, "Re: Writing tonight on your book, Penny...," Email message to author, June 1, 2006.

2. Andrew Buncombe and Oliver Duff, "The Life and Death of an Iraq Veteran Who Could Take No More," *The Independent*, January 25, 2006, http://news.independent.co.uk/world/americas/article340826.ece.

3. Doug Barber, "Spc Douglas Barber: PTSD-Every Soldier's Personal WAR!," *Tales of the Freeway Blogger*, January 9, 2005, http://freewayblogger.blogspot.com/2006/01/suicide-note.html.

4. Buncombe and Duff, "The Life and Death of an Iraq Veteran Who Could Take No More."

5. Crawford, *The Last True Story I'll Ever Tell*, 220.

6. Ann Scott Tyson, "U.S. Casualties in Iraq Rise Sharply," *Washington Post*, October 8, 2006, http://www.washingtonpost.com/wp-dyn/content/article/2006/10/07/AR2006100700907.html.

7. Karen M. Pavlicin, *Surviving Deployment: A Guide for Military Families*, (St. Paul: Elva Resa Publishing, 2003), xxvi.

8. Cathy Shufro, "The Unseen Wounds of War," *Yale Medicine*, Autumn 2005, http://yalemedicine.yale.edu/ym_au05/war.html.

9. Lee Hill Kavanaugh, "Return to civilian life is hard for vets—and those they left behind," *Kansas City Star*, June 8, 2006.

10. Erin Emery, "War vets' mental health has police on alert," *Denver Post*, September 17, 2006, http://www.denverpost.com/search/ci_4351441.

11. Ibid.

12. Shufro, "The Unseen Wounds of War."

13. Eric T. Dean, Jr., *Shook Over Hell: Post-Traumatic Stress, Vietnam, and the Civil War*, (Cambridge: Harvard University Press, 1997), 5.

14. Paul Rieckhoff, *Chasing Ghosts: A Soldier's Fight for America from Baghdad to Washington*, (New York: NAL, 2006), 261.

15. "Talk of the Nation: Science Friday," *National Public Radio*, April 25, 2003, http://www.sciencefriday.com/kids/sfkc20030425-1.html

16. Tick, *War and Soul*, 17.

17. Gabriel. *No More Heroes*, 155–156.

18. Robert B. Edgerton, *Like Lions They Fought: The Zulu War and the Last Black Empire in South Africa*, (New York: Ballatine Books, 1988), 45.

19. Tick, *War and Soul*, 209.

20. Peter J. Murphy, "Postdeployment Support," *Military Stress and Performance*, 142.

21. David Read Johnson, et. al., "The Impact of the Homecoming Reception on the Development of Posttraumatic Stress Disorder: The West Haven Homecoming Stress Scale (WHHSS)," *Journal of Traumatic Stress* 10 (1997), 260–261.

22. James Janega and Aamer Madhani, "Postwar life is anything but normal" *Chicago Tribune*, October 20, 2006, 10

23. Alexandra Marks, "Back From Iraq – And Suddenly Out On the Streets," *Christian Science Monitor*, February 8, 2005.

24. Department of Veteran Affairs, "Homeless Veterans: Overview of Homelessness," October 12, 2006, http://www1.va.gov/homeless/page.cfm?pg=1.

25. National Coalition for Homeless Veterans, "Facts and Media: Media Information," http://www.nchv.org/media.cfm.

26. Rose Aguilar, "Gimme Shelter," *Alternet*, February, 8, 2005, http://www.alternet.org/waroniraq/21191/.

27. National Coalition for Homeless Veterans, "Facts and Media: Media Information."

28. Cassie Feldman, "For Some Vets, A Home Isn't Waiting," *Newsday*, November 13, 2005.

29. Alexandra Marks, "Back From Iraq – And Suddenly Out On the Streets," *Christian Science Monitor*, February 8, 2005.

30. Verena Dobnik, "A welcome home missing for many returning military," *Houston Chronicle,* July 5, 2006.

31. James Janega and Aamer Madhani, "Postwar life is anything but normal" *Chicago Tribune,* October 20, 2006, 10

32. Rose Aguilar, "Gimme Shelter."

33. National Coalition for Homeless Veterans, "Facts and Media: VA Announces Grants for Homeless Programs," November 13, 2006, http://www.nchv.org/news_article.cfm?id=261.

34. oofer, "Re: ilona," December 22, 2005, Online posting, #2 | Returning Vet PTSD: One Wife's Story, http://www.dailykos.com/story/2005/12/22/13722/073

35. Donna St. George, "Iraq War May Add Stress for Past Vets," *Washington Post,* June 20, 2006, http://www.washingtonpost.com/wp-dyn/content/article/2006/06/19/AR2006061901400.html; "Cleland Treated For Post Traumatic Stress," *WSBTV-Atlanta,* August 28, 2006, http://www.wsbtv.com/news/9747929/detail.html.

36. Jim Starowicz, "Here Ya Go Ilona," Email message to author, September 17, 2006.

37. Stefanie Pelkey, "OEF/OIF PTSD Book – Permission Requested," Email message to author, June 28, 2006. Learn more about Pelkey's work at www.homefronthealing.org/index.html.

38. Leo Shane III, "Widow warns of postwar stress issues," July 28, 2005, *Stars & Stripes,* http://www.stripesonline.com/article.asp?section=104&article=29811&archive=true.

39. Lucey, *OEF/OIF Written History Survey Form.*